MAN

MORAL AND PHYSICAL:

OR THE

INFLUENCE OF HEALTH AND DISEASE

ON

RELIGIOUS EXPERIENCE.

BY THE

REV. JOSEPH H. JONES, D. D.

PASTOR OF THE SIXTH PRESBYTERIAN CHURCH, PHILADELPHIA.

Non ignara mali miseris succurrere disco.

Ἀδύνατον, κακῶς ψυχῆς ἐχούσης,
Μὴ οὐ καὶ σῶμα αὐτῇ συνοίσειν.

PHILADELPHIA:
WILLIAM S. & ALFRED MARTIEN
606 CHESTNUT STREET.
1860.

ERRATA.

On page 42, line tenth from top, for *Aretœus* read *Aretœus.*

On page 112, line sixth from top, for *passis* read *possis.*

CONTENTS.

CHAPTER I.

CHAPTER II.

CHAPTER III.

CHAPTER IV.

PREFACE.

A devout physician once told a friend of the writer, that "he never knew a triumphant death when the disease of the pious patient was below the diaphragm." This remark may be taken in a broader sense than its author intended, and from which we should earnestly dissent; but it recognizes a power of our bodily maladies to control and pervert the healthful functions of the mind, which none are more concerned to know than they who have the cure of souls. Within the range of almost every pastor's charge of moderate extent, cases of spiritual distress are occurring to which he can minister no relief; they lie beyond the reach of any remedies to which he can resort. The latent cause is the morbid condition of the physical part, which brings them legitimately within the province of the physician. On the other hand, the instances are scarcely less multiplied, in which all the science and skill of the healing art are impotent, till the thorn is extracted from the conscience. The influence of physical agents on moral states, moreover, is too little understood or heeded by the instructors of our children. They do not sufficiently consider the connection between intellect and morality, or between sensation and thought. "The study and the statistics of mental disease teach a fearful lesson concerning the giant evils resulting from ignorant mismanagement of the body in relation to the mind and the moral nature."

It has been intimated by judicious friends, that our smaller work on this subject first published, would have been made more instructive and extensively useful by a considerable amplification. The last two letters that we ever received from our lamented friend and correspondent, Dr. James W. Alexander, related mainly to its reproduction and enlargement "on several points," which he thought "should be treated more fully." None of all our friends ever expressed a deeper interest in the subject of this book, nor helped us more by their counsel, than the late Doctors Alexander, both father and son. The removal of the former, *like a shock of corn in his season*, though causing wide spread sorrow, did not take us by surprise.

> Multis ille bonis flebilis, occidit;
> Nulli flebilior, quam mihi.

The death of the latter, *in his full strength*, and at the time of so great and increasing usefulness, was painfully abrupt, and seemed to be premature. He was taken from a large circle of admirers, whose memory lingers on their irreparable loss, with the mournful reflection expressed in that "exquisite inscription of Shenstone's," whose aroma no translation can preserve,

> Heu! quanto minus est cum reliquis versari, quam tui meminisse!

They almost forget the living in their reminiscences of the dead.

We have so far respected the suggestions of our advisers as to add to what was presented in the prior edition many interesting facts, which, however familiar to persons conversant with the standard works on Physiology and Hygiene, will be new to others. Changes have been made in other respects by additions and various modifications, especially under the heads of TEMPTATIONS and COUNSELS, which have materially increased its size, and made it more conducive to the purpose for which it was written. The author makes no pretension to originality or deep thinking, nor to such an acquaintance with psychology, or physical science, as a more thorough and enlightened discussion of the subject requires. So far as the thoughts of others have been approved, and were adapted to the purpose of the writer, they have been adopted, often in their own language, and are here acknowledged in general, to supersede the necessity of multiplied marginal references and marks of quotation. The authors of certain well-written papers on subjects kindred to this, in the Literary and Theological Review, the Biblical Repertory, and Christian Spectator, will perceive our obligations to them. Doctors George and John Cheyne, Combe, Good, Moore, Broussais, Burrows, Rush, Dunglison, Brigham, Hall, and Esquirol, have been consulted, especially Dr. James Johnson, justly called "the ablest and most effective writer of the age on every subject to which his attention was directed." Little is left for a successor to glean in any field of medical research after having been reaped by him. We have also had much assistance from "the soundest and ablest medical periodical in the English language"—the Medico-Chirurgical Review. As reference will be found in the present work to certain writers on subjects akin to that of which it treats, we give the titles of a few for the guidance of any who may have leisure and inclination to read them. In addition to those already named, we would mention Pritchard, Pinel, Prout; Voison on the Moral and Physical Causes of Mental Maladies; Tissot on the Health of Men of Letters; Hitchcock's Lectures on Diet, Regimen, and Employment; Shepherd's Sincere Convert; and Robe on Religious Melancholy. Most of these, of course, view the subject of which they treat, as philosophers or men of science; but those who have access to the older English divines will find that questions of casuistry, spiritual troubles, evidences of grace, &c., are discussed with great ability, and are made far more prominent and important in them than they are in the theological works of times more modern. The writings of the Rev. Timothy Rogers, several times quoted in the ensuing pages, are peculiarly instructive to persons labouring under spiritual distress, as having been dictated by his own experience. Those who cannot get this rare book will find a choice sample of its counsels in the fourth chapter of Dr. Archibald Alexander's "Thoughts on Religious Experience." From this interesting work, as well as from the "Discourse of Mr. Rogers on Trouble of Mind and the Disease of Melancholy," we have received important aid.

The writer has been gratified with the favour shown to his imperfect treatise by the press, both secular and religious; and especially with testimonials, through private channels, that it has proved useful in ministering relief to some of that class for whom it was principally designed. That the same beneficent results may follow this enlarged edition is the sincere desire of the author, as it ought to be his paramount motive in preparing it for publication.

MAN, MORAL AND PHYSICAL.

CHAPTER I.

CONNECTION BETWEEN THE MATERIAL AND SPIRITUAL PARTS IN MAN.

How poor, how rich, how abject, how august,
How complicate, how wonderful is man!—YOUNG.

"I WILL praise Thee," says David, "for I am fearfully and wonderfully made." How far the Psalmist understood the full import of his words, or was acquainted with the wonderful mechanism of man to which he alludes, we do not presume to know. It is enough to say, that the terms which he uses are most appropriate and descriptive, as has been abundantly proved by the researches of physiology. But curious and fearful as is the structure of the material part, there is displayed far more of the wisdom and greatness of God in the creation and endowments of the soul; and although we are accustomed to speak familiarly of both, as

2

if they were well understood, yet there is scarcely a term which we employ which is not rather a symbol of what we do not know, than an exponent of what we do. The mystery of the Trinity is not more inexplicable than is the connection that subsists between the body and the soul of man. The most that we know of either, is derived from the results which flow from such an union. As we infer the being and co-operation of the three persons in the Godhead, from the nature and the benefits of redemption, by which this triune existence is implied, so we become assured that we have a spirit as well as a body, from their acts or motions, which we feel. We know nothing of the substance of which either is composed, nor of the mode in which the two are linked together. The attempts of science to reach and explain these ultimate facts, have not amounted to even an approximation. Whatever has been written concerning the locality of the soul, the time of its entrance into the body, the mode by which it acts upon or governs it, and the avenue through which it escapes at death, is but little more than speculation and conjecture. Dr. Abercrombie says, "we talk about matter, and we talk about mind; we speculate concerning materiality and immateriality, until we argue ourselves into a kind of belief that we understand something of the subject. The truth is, that we understand nothing." We really know but little more than a few facts in relation to both, which are dscoverable by their respective qualities and attributes; such as that the two are closely united; that what is called the nervous system is the medium of communication between them; so that they exert a strong reciprocal influence upon each other; that when the one is afflicted, it always has the sympathy of the other. They, therefore, have been employed more wisely, who, leaving the former as among the inscrutable things of God, have endeavoured to make a practical improvement of the latter. It is a subject that so intimately blends with all that conduces to the enjoyment and usefulness of life, as well as its continuance, that it is of the highest importance for all to understand it, and to none is such knowledge more needful than to the official teachers of religion.

It is proposed at this time to offer a few thoughts on this interesting topic, more with a view to awaken the attention, and invite the pen of others, than to furnish all that is needed. Indeed, such a work as the exigency of the Church has long demanded, is not likely to be accomplished by "any one who is not furnished with a suitable education, theological and medical, profoundly and experimentally acquainted with the Scriptures, fond of research, and gifted with good powers of generalization and induction."

For those who wish to pursue the subject in its pathological bearings, or as one of the departments of physiology, there are numerous medical treatises, both domestic and foreign, which are easily accessible. What we have to offer in the following chapters is little more than the result of some observation, and the few years' experience of a pastor. It is intended to furnish, in a portable form and size, a tract for the benefit of Christians of an unequal and fluctuating experience, produced by physical causes, though not suspected perhaps by themselves, nor their spiritual advisers.

It has already been said, that much that pertains to the nature of the connection between the flesh and the spirit is a mystery which science has tried in vain to explore. It has proceeded so far as to discover in the human fabric, certain delicate white threads, leading from the brain and spinal marrow to every part of the body. It has also been ascertained that by means of these nerves (as they are called from the Latin term *nervus*, a string) sensations are conveyed from each of the organs of sense to the brain; moreover, that these are the channels of communication between the mind and the body, as is proved by the well-known fact, that if one of the nerves of the arm or leg be sundered, all power of that limb is lost; if another be cut, sensation is no longer transmitted through the arm to the mind. The branches and ramifications of the nerves are so numerous and so generally diffused, that they have a virtual omnipresence throughout the animal fabric.

Though diminishing in size as they approach their places of termination, so that at length they become invisible to the naked eye, yet they lose none of their exquisite sensibility. The point of the finest needle cannot be brought into contact with the skin in any part of the body without detecting the presence of a nerve. The sensation caused by ever so delicate a touch upon the most attenuated branch is imparted to a larger, then to a larger still, and with electric rapidity to all; so that the remotest part is instantly conscious of the impression. This kind of correlation, by which different organs of the body are affected by impressions made upon one, through the commerce of the nerves, is called "sympathy." This mysterious intercourse is rendered more complete and effective by the agency of the intercostal or "sympathetic nerve," which, passing through the innumerable branches and plexuses, is the common channel of communicating with them all. Such is that fearful and wonderful department of the human economy called the NERVOUS SYSTEM—the great organ of thought, feeling, and voluntary motion. How much, then, must the enjoyment of life, as well as its usefulness, depend on its healthful condition! Nor is it the least wonderful of the whole, when we examine into the various functions of the nerves, and the perpetual irritations and violence to which they are exposed, that the nervous economy is not more frequently deranged than it is.

Anatomists tell us, that when these little threads become diseased, there is no perceptible change in their size, shape, colour, nor appearance. Even when the power of transmitting sensation is lost, nutrition still goes on, and the nerves remain as large in a paralyzed as in a healthy limb. Before a patient dies, they resist mortification longer than most parts of the body, and, after death, decay more slowly. This explains, in part, how it is that nervous diseases, which are often so prolonged, do not more impair the physical strength, nor seem to abridge the life of the sufferer.

With respect to the actual nature of the nervous force, we offer no opinion, nor quote the conjectures of others. The notion that obtained for a while among some physiologists, that it was identical with the electric power, has been generally abandoned in the present day. In what way, therefore, this communication between the brain, the spinal marrow, and the nerves is effected; how the volitions and conceptions of the mind are conveyed on these delicate material conductors—whether by tremors or vibrations, like the cords of a musical instrument, or, as Hippocrates and Galen supposed, by a fine ethereal fluid, elaborated in the organ of the brain, or by neither—what is their specific substance or construction, by which they are made not only vehicles of thought, but instruments of exquisite pleasure or pain, are among the questions that have been a constant source of hypothesis in past ages, but which neither reason nor revelation has answered. It is quite probable that neither our happiness nor our usefulness would be increased by a knowledge of the essence of mind and matter, and that enough is known from their various phenomena to answer every practical purpose. With that class of them which we are about to consider, the world of course have been more or less familiar ever since the fall subjected man to disease, and made the earthly part a clog, while it gave it such ascendency over the heavenly. But in regard to those morbid results of this connection, which are technically called "nervous," it has frequently been said, that, to a great extent, they are a penalty for an abuse of the multiplied blessings of civilized life. Among savage tribes, such affections are scarcely known, and they are very rare among those whose pursuits are active, and connected with habitual exposure. But they seem to have increased just in proportion as nations have advanced in outward prosperity and in intellectual refinement. Hence it is easily understood why medicine was no more diligently cultivated among the ancients, and how it happened that the first physician of eminence, who has been called the "father of medicine," should have lived within less than five hundred years before Christ. In the early ages of the world, there was comparatively little occasion for a profession that is now so highly honoured, and which is so indispensable to the health and happiness of society. The simplicity of manners which prevailed, plainness of diet, temperance, and activity in rural occupations, were productive of a degree of health and vigour which are hardly known at present. How far the great age of man, until shortened by a divine decree, was the result of natural causes, we do not presume to say; but the progress of the healing art has marked, with a good degree of accuracy, in successive ages, the increase of luxury and excessive sensual indulgence.

"Had it not been," Dr. Cheyne says, "for the lewdness, luxury, and intemperate gratification of the passions and appetites which first ruined and spoiled the constitution of the fathers, whereby they could communicate only a diseased, crazy, and untunable carcass to their sons, there had never happened so much sickness, pain, and misery, so unhappy lives, and such wretched ends, as we now behold among men." The records of prisons and almshouses prove that physical vices are not only perpetuated in the offspring of the guilty parent, but they originate mental deformities. Three-fourths of the idiotic in a Massachusetts' Charity were found to be of parents, one or both of whom were drunken. From an examition of juvenile delinquents at Parkhurst, by Mr. Kay Shuttleworth, it appeared that the majority were found deficient in physical organization. Mr. Coleridge says, that the history of a man for the months that precede his birth, would probably be far more interesting, and contain events of greater moment than all that follow it.

I. THE SACRED WRITINGS.

That these should furnish but little instruction on the subject of the present discussion, however important to so large a proportion of modern believers, is easily accounted for. This has fallen rather within the province of that science which has grown out of the changed circumstances of man, especially the great degeneracy in his habits of living. But while we discover in the Bible comparatively few of the elements of many modern theories concerning this union of the soul and body, and the moral results, yet they contain records of the experience and exercises of the religious, and of others, which afford many exemplifications of the fact. Such is supposed by some to have been the distressing affection of Saul, ascribed to an *evil spirit from God*, the successive paroxysms of which were allayed by the music of the son of Jesse. Stackhouse thinks, that it proceeded from deep depression of spirits, or black bile inflamed, and that he was rather hypochondriac than possessed. Agreeable to this bad complexion of body, was the natural temper of his mind.

Another example is quoted in the case of the Psalmist himself, when, in one of his sacred songs, his harp is tuned to strains of the deepest melancholy, and he mournfully sings: *My soul refused to be comforted. I remembered God, and was troubled; I complained, and my spirit was overwhelmed: I am so troubled that I cannot speak. Will the Lord cast off for ever? and will he be favourable no more? Is his mercy clean gone for ever? Hath God forgotten to be gracious?* And then he adds, *I said this is my infirmity;* an expression which means, as understood by some, that he suspects the cause of his great depression to be physical, or to proceed from the state of the body.

Another illustration of this connection, and the influence of the material part over the spiritual, has been drawn from the language of the Saviour in his gentle rebuke of the lethargy of the disciples in the garden of Gethsemane. That they should have fallen asleep under such circumstances, appeared to themselves to admit of no apology, and they did not attempt it. But on being awaked by their Master, he kindly remarked, *the spirit is willing, but the flesh is weak.* The delinquency was to be ascribed, not so much to the state of their heart, as to bodily fatigue; implying, as is commonly understood, a mild reproof, at the same time that it evinces the disposition of Christ to regard it as evidence more of natural infirmity than of guilt. The same injurious influence of the earthly part is recognized by the apostle Paul, in those numerous passages of his writings in which he so graphically describes the conflict between the flesh and the spirit: *I know that in me, that is, in my flesh, there dwelleth no good thing. I delight in the law of God, after the inner man, but I see another law in my members warring against the law of my mind, bringing me*, &c. In another place, he ascribes the inability of the law to justify, not to itself, but to a weakness *through the flesh.* We are aware that the term *flesh* here is used in a figurative sense, to signify the remainder of natural corruption which still adheres to the man, even after his moral state has become changed by regenerating grace. But the passages are none the less suited to our purpose, inasmuch as they imply that the organs of sense are made the instruments through which the corruption of our nature is developed, and its operation felt upon the spiritual man. In this connection, it may be observed, that the writings of the Fathers contain numerous quotations from the serious minded heathen, that show a striking coincidence with the opinions of Paul on the subject of depravity, and especially the prejudicial influence of the body. Cicero's remark is familiar to many—that men are brought into life by nature, as a step-mother, with a frail and infirm body, with a soul prone to divers lusts. And what but this doctrine of physical influence is perverted and caricatured in that motley mixture of Christianity and Persian philosophy contained in the system of the Manicheans of the third century of the Christian era, concerning the two principles of good and evil—the former of which is represented as the creator of the soul of man, and the latter of his body.

II. THE TESTIMONY OF SCIENCE.

If what the Scriptures contain on this subject amounts only to hints or implications, rather than positive declarations, our light is abundant when we come to the testimony of science. The connection and influence of which we speak, have been proved and illustrated with great clearness by those who have examined the structure of the human system, its capacities and functions, organic, intellectual, and moral. They have not failed to see how much the state of the mind and moral feelings has to do with the induction, the persistence, and final issue of many maladies. This connection is as fully implied in the abuses of this truth, as it is taught in its legitimate uses. Thus it has been made to furnish the basis of materialism under the milder, and, as understood and taught by many, the innocent forms of cranioscopy, craniology, phrenology, &c., as well as of that grosser system of Lawrence, which makes the soul of man a mere chymical combination, which contends that it is not a spiritual substance, distinct from his body, but that the principle within him which thinks, is material; and that reasoning and reflection are functions of organized matter; which gravely tells him that he grows like a vegetable, or accretes like a crystal; or is attracted and repulsed like a particle of iron exposed to magnetic influence: That his brain secretes thought, as his liver secretes bile; that believing and disbelieving are acts of the soul, as is tasting of the body, and one is as destitute of any moral character as the other; and therefore, that it is as absurd to suppose a man blamable for being an atheist, as for being afflicted with an attack of the gout. That organized differs from inorganized matter, merely by the addition of certain properties, such as sensibility and irritability, which are called vital. The masses of matter which constitute the several parts of the animal frame are endowed according to the respective functions or purposes which they are to execute, and life is the general result of their exercise. Upon this hypothesis, the human frame is nothing more than "a barrel-organ, possessing a systematic arrangement of parts, played upon by peculiar powers, and executing particular pieces or purposes. Life is the music produced by the general assemblage, or result of the harmonious action. As long as either the vital or mechanical instrument is wound up by a regular supply of food, or of the winch, so long the music will continue; but both are worn out by their own action; and when the machine will no longer work, the life has the same close as the music;

——— redit in nihilum, quod fuit ante nihil.

That, back to nothing goes, which nothing was before.

That such sentiments as these are as directly at variance with sound science as they are with revealed religion, it is gratuitous to assert. In admitting, as we have done, that this inexplicable union of the body and soul may involve many truths which have not yet been discovered, we do not concede that it warrants any such atheistic corollaries as this. It would be easy to show, that although commended by names of some notoriety, yet such a materialism is "a logical absurdity, and a total misconception of the first principles of philosophical inquiry." But as it is our purpose in this disquisition to keep within the province of Christian casuistry, we think it better, in passing, rather to hint at than quote, as freely as we might, the illustrations of the present head, which are furnished by physiology. Yet all may safely be granted to the influence of the flesh upon the spirit, which truth requires, without affording the smallest ground for those shocking conclusions.

The great vital organs of the human system, such as the brain, stomach, liver, &c., may seem to act as mechanically as the hand, the ear, or the tongue, yet the health of the mind is much affected by the healthful state of this apparatus of the body. Notice, first,

THE BRAIN. We know and admit, that the operations of the intellect are closely allied to that soft whitish mass, or viscus, lodged beneath the arched bone of the head, which is called the brain. Thus a blow which depresses a portion of the skull upon the brain, will cause a derangement or suspension of the mind's operations until such pressure is removed. A man at the battle of Waterloo had a small portion of his skull-bone beat in upon the brain, to the depth of half an inch. This caused volition and sensation to cease, and he was nearly in a lifeless state. So soon as the depressed portion of bone was raised from the brain, the man immediately arose, dressed himself, became perfectly rational, and recovered rapidly.

It has been discovered that whatever produces mental excitement, increases the flow of blood to the head, and thus augments the size and power of the brain; just as exertion of the limbs enlarges and strengthens their muscles. Sir Astley Cooper had a patient whose skull was so imperfect as to enable him to examine the movements of the brain. "I distinctly saw," Sir Astley says, "that the pulsation of the brain was regular and slow; but at this time he was agitated by some opposition to his wishes, and directly the blood was sent with increased force to his brain, and the pulsations became frequent and violent."

A case more interesting still, mentioned by Dr. Caldwell, was a female who had lost a large portion of the skull and dura mater by disease. When she was in a dreamless sleep, her brain was motionless; when her sleep was imperfect, and disturbed by dreams, her brain protruded from the cranium. In vivid dreams, reported as such by herself, the protrusion was considerable; and when perfectly awake, especially if engaged in active thought, or sprightly conversation, it was much greater.

It is known that the brain of an adult of ordinary intellect is comparatively large, weighing about three and a half pounds, often a little less. In some persons of uncommon mind, it has been known to be much greater. The brain of Byron, for instance, is said to have weighed four and a half pounds, and that of Baron Cuvier four pounds thirteen ounces and a half. On the other hand, the brain of an idiot does not exceed in size that of a child a year old, or between one and two pounds in weight. It has been proved by measurement, that the heads of great thinkers frequently continue to increase until the subjects are fifty years of age, and long after the other portions of the system have ceased to enlarge. This was true of Bonaparte, whose head, though small in youth, in after life became enormous. The reverse is known to occur in cases of protracted insanity; not only the brain diminishes, but the skull itself has often sensibly contracted, as is mentioned of Dean Swift, who, in the latter part of his life, sunk into a state of mental imbecility, a distressing calamity, of which he appears to have had a presentiment, having predicted "that he would first die at top."

It is vain then to deny that this wonderful part of the body has much to do with the manifestations of mind, though we know of no warrant for the strange conceit of the older physiologists, that there is some central spot in that organ where all the messages of the nerves are ultimately reported, and whence all the orders of the will are issued; or for the figment of Descartes, that the peculiar seat of the mind is the pineal gland. Nor is it incredible, that a different combination of the physical elements of the man may occasion a corresponding difference in the character and qualities of the mind; that a genius for poetry or mathematics, for painting or music, may be connected with a peculiar arrangement or disposition of some particles in the animal economy; in other words, that the earthen vessel is so constructed in some particulars, which escape the eye of the anatomist, as to form a different mould, or give a peculiar shape to the mind, according to the sphere of usefulness for which it is designed by its Creator. All this may be true, and not conflict with the teachings of revelation. Indeed, for aught we know to the contrary, it is comprehended in what the Psalmist calls the "fearful and wonderful" construction of man. But in what way the power of thought is originated, or how it is affected by the matter in which it seems to be lodged, is perhaps as profound a secret to Gabriel as it is to us; while the facts by which the truth itself is demonstrated, are, many of them, as affecting as they are familiar. Is the body attacked and prostrated by disease, it is sure of the sympathy of its spiritual partner, which is often reduced to the feebleness of infancy by the debility of the former. Its perceptions become obtuse, the memory fails, the power of attention is gone, as we are often painfully admonished by discovering that the conversation and counsels which were given to the sick, their confessions, and promises, and prayers, are all forgotten on their recovery. Perhaps it is not recollected even, that we were once at their bedside and addressed them. But the connection is not less intimate between the mind and

THE STOMACH. Whether this sympathy takes place through the medium of the blood-vessels, the nerves, or both, we do not know. Nothing is made more familiar by experience than the fact, that the vigorous action of the former depends, in a great degree, upon the sound condition of the latter. Some assert that the brain, as the common sensorium to which all sensations are ultimately referred, is the first to become sensible to the disorder of the stomach. That, "like two friends in harmonious co-operation, they mutually support each other in health; but, in disease, like sworn enemies, they act and react upon each other with the most destructive malignity." Who has not observed, without the aid of books or physicians to suggest it, that whatever painfully affects his mind, and disturbs its equanimity, takes away his appetite for food, or the power to digest it, and causes more or less disquietude in the stomach. For this reason, a strong excitement of the mind is often one of the surest remedies for this uneasiness. No man, perhaps, ever had an appetite for food under the full influence of the depressing passions, such as fear or grief. He may eat from persuasion, or from a sense of duty, but he eats without desire or a craving sense of hunger. Hence, those who are suddenly deprived of their senses by an overwhelming and unexpected evil, pass days and nights without food of any kind, each sufferer feeling with King Lear,

> When the mind's free
> The body's delicate: the tempest in my mind
> Doth from my senses take all feeling else
> Save what beats there.

Dr. Brigham says: "One day, when about to sit down to dinner, with an appetite whetted by five or six hours' exercise, a letter was put into my hands announcing the death of a friend to whom I felt strongly attached. The consequence was an instantaneous loss of appetite, which continued for two or three days." A stern look, and a very few reproachful words from Henry VIII. gave the ambitious Woolsey a fit of indigestion which destroyed the Cardinal's life.

The stomach, in its turn, reacts upon the mind, causing confusion of thought, defect of memory, and of the power of abstraction—not

4

to mention despondency, irascibility, and other kinds of morbid mental disturbance, by which the sufferer is made ineffably wretched. Hence dyspepsia, that malady so Protean in its forms, once generally thought to be a disease originating always in the stomach, is now considered by many of the most intelligent of the faculty as primarily a disease of the brain and nervous system, perpetuated by mental excitement, especially in the case of students. Thus it has been observed, that persons who are in the habit of strongly employing their mental faculties shortly after taking food, are more or less subject to this affection. In such a case, the nervous energy required for the process of digestion, instead of being expended upon the stomach, is wasted upon the intellectual organs. Aristotle informs us that all the great men of his time were hypochondriacs; that "they had cultivated their mind at the expense of their body."

Nor is the force of the morbid impulse proceeding from the brain wholly exhausted upon the stomach, but often reaches to

THE LUNGS AND HEART—causing diseased

action in both. The acute pain sometimes felt in the region of the heart, a tremulous or fluttering sensation there, interruptions of the pulse, and palpitations, which the alarmed sufferer is ready to ascribe to organic disease, are very often symptoms only of "gastric derangement, which has been generated by the morbific influence of the mind."

But none of the viscera of the body better show its alliance to the mind, or illustrate and establish this mysterious influence of the body on the mind, than the

LIVER. What are all the uses of this organ in the human economy, is still a subject of inquiry. The main service which it performs, so far as is generally understood, is merely the secretion daily of a few ounces of bile. But when we consider its dimensions—the largest gland of any kind in the human system—the number and size of its parts, and its peculiar structure, we cannot resist the impression that this great constituent of the vital mechanism is used for a higher purpose than this. And hence the opinion has obtained, both among the ancients and moderns, that the liver has a powerful influence on the temperament, the mental functions, and the passions of the man, and thus affecting his moral and religious feelings. We presume to offer no solution of the fact, nor even a conjecture, why a certain class of mental phenomena should be developed by the condition of this particular gland; why the liver should exhibit its affinities for that which is gloomy and sad, rather than the lungs or heart? But the fact is witnessed every day, that such is the power of many of the depressing passions when suddenly excited, that they cause a gush of bile into the system at large, which gives a yellow tinge to the eye, and overcasts the mind with the most rueful forebodings and ineffable despondency. Why it should cause this mental dejection, is just as inexplicable as is the hopeful, buoyant spirit of the hectic patient, whose more desperate malady is seated in his lungs. The contrast is remarkable, whatever may be the cause. While in the last stage of consumption the sufferer is cheerful and incredulous as to the issue which is so obvious to others, the man labouring under disease of the liver is often oppressed with a heaviness of heart which repels relief from any suggestion of reason or the consolations of religion. The classical reader will recollect the frightful story of the miserable Tityus, as told by both Homer and Virgil, who, for his nameless crime, was condemned to be eternally tormented by the preying of a vulture upon his liver, which was supernaturally reproduced as fast as consumed.

> Rostroque immanis vultur obunco,
> Immortale jecur tundens.
>
> A huge vulture, with his hooky beak,
> Pouncing his immortal liver.—*Davidson.*

Whether our poets designed that fable should receive a physiological gloss, and were prompted, in part, by their own morbid experiences or not, it is certainly a most graphic allegory, descriptive at once of the seat, the intensity, and hopelessness of that unspeakable wretchedness which so often proceeds from a diseased condition of this organ. Such would seem to have been the opinion of Lucretius, who, in giving the moral of various heathen fables, furnishes the following interpretation of this, as translated by Dryden.

> No Tityus torn by vultures lies in hell,
> Nor could the lobes of his rank liver swell
> To that prodigious mass for their eternal meal.
> But he's the Tityus, who by love oppressed,
> Or tyrant passions preying on his breast,
> And ever anxious thoughts, is robbed of rest.

Hippocrates, Galen, Aretœus, and other illustrious ancients, were accustomed to describe a great variety of mental disease under the general term "melancholy," because they believed a pensive and desponding state of the mind to arise from a superabundance of "black bile," the literal meaning of the compound word "melancholy." Others supposed the hidden cause of this mental depression to be the

SPLEEN—and hence, "to be spleeny," as descriptive of the gloomy and disconsolate, has come down to us traditionally as a saying of antiquity. What is the use of this spongy viscus has never been determined. Dr. Good says various hypotheses have been offered by learned men; but they are hypotheses, and nothing more. Archdeacon Paley thinks it is employed as needful in the package of the animal mass. It is possible, he says, that the spleen may be "merely a stuffing, a soft cushion to fill up a vacancy or hollow, which, unless occupied, would leave the package loose and unsteady." The same opinion concerning the influence of the liver in producing emotions of sadness is conveyed in the word "hypochondriac," applied by the ancients to the melancholy, and which has been domesticated by the moderns. Every reader who can analyse the term, knows that it designates the position of this organ, *υπο χονδρον, under the cartilage.* Thus the opinion obtained early, that by some mysterious generation, affections of this sombre cast were the offspring of the liver.

The writer is indebted to a lady of genius, and various accomplishments of both mind and person, for a critical remark and suggestion in relation to the subject of hepatic influence, as furnished by her own experience. She is favourably known to the literary and religious community by several instructive and interesting works, and has paid the common penalty of the studious in those physical ailments which are too often the price of their success. She had very soon discovered that the fluctuations in her animal spirits, religious enjoyment, and spiritual exercises generally; the changes in her temper, mental energy, and cheerfulness, to which she is painfully subject, were symptomatic of a corresponding change in the condition of this sensitive organ. But the exhibition of some simple remedy, by which its healthful functions are restored, brings back at once her elastic freedom of thought and cheerfulness.

The preceding illustrations of the close connection between the spiritual man and the material, are doubtless ample for the ordinary reader. But in view of the grave moral uses to which this interesting truth is to be applied in our subsequent remarks, we will presume on the reader's indulgence while we adduce a few to exemplify the power of the passions as disturbers of the healthy action of our bodies. Some of these, it is known, retard the circulation of the blood, which, on the contrary, is accelerated by opposite emotions that are stronger and more vigorous. Who has failed to notice how the heart palpitates, and the "pulse gallops," when the mind is excited by

LOVE. When Antiochus the Syrian was ill of an occult disease which threatened his life, the cause of it was undiscoverable until betrayed to his physicians by their observing that his pulse suddenly became irregular whenever Stratonice entered the room. It then appeared that love for her was the cause of his illness. This was immediately told to his royal father, who willingly gave her to his son, that his immoderate passion might not cause his death. Not less operative is the influence of

HOPE. What fact is better established by the teachings, as well as the experience of the medical profession, than that the success of surgical operations, and the results of medicine, are materially affected by the hope or despair that preponderates in the mind of the patient.

Surgeons in the army have noticed a marked contrast between the mortality among the wounded of a victorious and that of a conquered army. The most severe and apparently desperate cases recover in the former, while hospital gangrene, erysipelas, typhus, and dysentery, usually decimate the latter. Even the lighter cases are comparatively slow in their recovery, and imperfect in their convalescence. After the great battle on the Mincio, 1859, between the French and Sardinians on the one side, and Austrians on the other, so disastrous to the latter, the defeated army retreated, followed by the victors. A description of the march of each army is given by two correspondents of the *London Times*, one of whom travelled with the successful host, the other with the defeated. The differences in views and statements of the same place, scenes, and events, is remarkable. The former are said to be marching through a beautiful and luxuriant country during the day, and at night encamping where they are supplied with an abundance of the best provisions, and all sorts of rural dainties.

There is nothing of war about the proceeding, except its stimulus and excitement. On the side of the poor Austrians it is just the reverse. In his letter of the same date, describing the same places, and a march over the same road, the writer can scarcely find words to set forth the sufferings, impatience, and disgust existing around him. What was pleasant to the former was intolerable to the latter. What made all this difference? asks the journalist. "One condition only; the French are victorious, the Austrians have been defeated. The contrast may convey a distinctive idea of the extent to which moral impressions affect the efficiency of the soldier."

When Dr. Rush was asked by a young man, his patient, supposed to be near his death in consumption, whether he might learn to play on the flute, the doctor told him yes, and at once said to his parents that he would get well. Parke tells us in his travels that one day, in his journey through the burning desert, exhausted with privations and fatigue, and ready, as he supposed, to die, he chanced at that moment to spy a tiny flower that had reared its head above the ground. "What!" thought he—"will that Providence which has watched over this humble plant, not care for me, who have been taught to regard him as a Father?" The thought revived his sinking spirits, and he immediately felt both his strength and his resolution to be greatly invigorated. Not less potent is the agency of

FEAR. How much has been said of its injurious influence as predisposing to disease, especially during the prevalence of epidemics! A curious experiment was tried in Russia with four murderers, who were placed, without knowing it, in separate beds, where four persons had died with cholera. They slept soundly and safely, none of them taking the disease. They were then put into beds, on which they were told that persons had just died of malignant cholera. The beds, however, were perfectly new, and had not been used at all. The result was, that three of them took the disease, and died within four hours.

During the prevalence of that appaling epidemic in the city of Philadelphia and vicinity, not a single case occurred among the inmates of the Cherry Hill prison, which was ascribed to the fact that the existence of that pestilence in their neighbourhood was effectually concealed from them until its severity had abated. Doubtless the freedom of physicians from fear is one of the main causes of the well-known immunity with which so many of them mingle among patients sick with the most contagious diseases. The efficacy of fear has been exhibited in instances of recovery from complaints which bade defiance to every means that science could devise. Both Doctors Batchelder and Rush mention cases of gout which were effectually dispelled by a sudden fright. An old man who for several years had suffered an annual attack of gout, was lying in one of these paroxysms, when his son, by some accident, drove the shaft of a wagon through the window of his room, with a terrific noise and a disastrous smashing of the glass. The shock was electrifying, and he leaped from his bed with

5

the agility of a boy, forgetting his crutches and cane, which were no longer needed.

By the same prophylactic aid of fear, Boerhaave once relieved a number of persons from epileptic fits, which were occasioned by witnessing the convulsions of others. In the hearing of these patients, he gave orders that hot irons should be applied to the first person who should be attacked. The expedient proved successful, and not one opportunity occurred for a resort to this frightful remedy. And who can doubt that most of the monomania which Dr. Moore calls the fashionable apology for murder, might be effectually prevented by the restraining agency of fear, if known that certain retribution would follow the crime.

Not long ago a man in New Hampshire was convicted of murder, committed in a state of partial derangement from strong drink. Just before his execution he acknowledged that his punishment was deserved, but added, that "had I known I should be hung for killing the man, I would have let him alone."

The teachings of Broussais respecting inflammation of the stomach, made such an impression on the minds, and so excited the fears of many, we are told, as to have greatly multiplied the cases in Paris at the time. Doctor John Hunter attributed the heart-disease, by which he ultimately died in a fit of passion, to his fear of having caught hydrophobia while dissecting the body of a patient who died of that disease. When Corvisart lectured at Paris on the heart, affections of that organ, whether real or imaginary, were greatly multiplied. He agrees with Testa, another writer on the same subject, that the feelings have great influence in changing the natural action of the heart, and producing disorder. The latter author considered the powerful and irregular operations of the passions as the most frequent cause of organic disease of the heart; which explains why this complaint was so much more common in Italy during seasons of political agitation, and especially in France at the time of the Revolution, than at any other period. The French *Journal of Medicine* records the case of an aged female, who, from agitation and fright, became black as a negro, from head to foot in a few hours. The same cause whitened the hair on half the head of a patient in the Pennsylvania Hospital, and on the whole head of Marie Antoinette, wife of Louis XVI., in a single night.

A correspondent of the *London Medical Times*, writing from India, February 19, 1858, says that a Sepoy of the Bengal army, having been made a prisoner, was brought before the authorities for examination. The man trembled violently; intense horror and despair were depicted on his face, and he seemed to be almost stupified with fear. The writer, who was present, adds, that within the space of half an hour his hair became gray on every portion of his head. "When first seen by us, it was the glossy jet-black of the Bengalee; his age was twenty-four. The attention of the bystanders was first attracted by the Sergeant, whose prisoner he was, exclaiming, 'he is turning gray!' and I, with several other persons, watched its progress. Gradually, but decidedly, the change went on, and a uniform gray colour was completed within the period above named."

A few years ago two young men attempted to rob an eagle's nest, high up on a cliff on the bank of the Hudson river, but several feet below the summit. One of them was let down in a basket, suspended by a rope, till he came opposite the nest. The eagle returned to protect her young, and in endeavouring to defend himself against her talons, the young man drew his knife, and in the contest accidentally cut all the strands of the rope but one. Meantime his companion was drawing him up to the summit, but he was so affected by fear at his perilous condition, that the next day his hair became as hoary as that of an old man.

The following case may be adduced, not merely for the illustration of our subject, but for the wholesome warning that it suggests against the vice of which it is a monitory register. A young man, twenty-three years old, came from the mines to San Francisco, with the intention of soon leaving the latter place for home. On the evening of his arrival, he, with his companions, visited the gambling saloons. After watching for a time the varied fortunes of a table, supposed to be undergoing the process of "tapping," from the continued success of those betting against the bank, the excitement overcame his better judgment, and he threw upon the "seven-spot" of a new deal, a bag which he said contained eleven hundred dollars—his all—the result of two years' privation and hard labour—exclaiming, with a voice trembling from intense excitement, "My home, or the mines!" As the dealer slowly resumed the drawing of his cards, his countenance, livid with fear of the inevitable fate that seems ever attendant upon the tapping process when once commenced, the writer, who was present, says: "I turned my eyes upon the young man who had staked his whole gains upon a card. Never shall I forget the impression made by his look of intense anxiety as he watched the cards as they fell from the dealer's hands. All the energies of his system seemed concentrated in the fixed gaze of his eyes, while the deadly pallor of his face bespoke the subdued action of his heart. All around seemed infected with the sympathetic powers of the spell; even the hitherto successful winners forgot their own stakes in the hazardous chance placed upon the issue of the bet. The cards are slowly told with the precision of high-wrought excitement. The seven-spot wins—the spell is broken—reaction takes place. The winner exclaims, with a deep-drawn sigh, 'I will never gamble again!' and was carried from the room in a deep swoon, from which he did not fully recover until the next morning; and then to know that the equivalent surrendered for his gain was the colour of his hair, now changed to a perfect white!" Not less sudden, nor less calamitous often, are the effects of

Grief. Father Chrysostom describes it as "a cruel torture of the soul, consuming the body, and gnawing the very heart." Melancthon says, "it strikes the heart, makes it flutter and pine away in great pain." It was believed that Philip V. of Spain died suddenly by the breaking of his heart on hearing of the hopeless defeat of his army near Plaisance. Dr.

Zimmerman states, that on opening the king's body the heart was found actually burst; so that, as Johnson says, the vulgar metaphorical expression of a "broken heart," is sometimes pathologically correct. What amazing results have followed a sudden paroxysm of

JOY. A woman in the city of New York heard that her husband and child were on board a ship that had been wrecked. Accustomed to go to the wharf from day to day, as if desirous of being nearer the beloved objects that were supposed to be buried beneath the sea, she suddenly beheld them landing from a vessel that had picked them up. The joy on seeing them safe was overwhelming. After the first salutation her reason fled, and from that time to the present she has not known them. She still sits on what she thinks the same rock where she used to bewail their fate, wringing her hands with ineffable distress; while every week the husband and son visit her, hoping to find a gleam of returning memory, but in vain.

Sophocles, Chilo, Juventius, Talma, and Fouquet, are said to have died from the excitement of excessive joy. Life was extinguished in a moment by a sudden surcharge of the brain with blood, causing apoplexy. How many have witnessed the withering power of

CHAGRIN, or SHAME. Rev. Daniel Baker tells the story of a young man, who several years ago was charged before an ecclesiastical court with an infamous crime, but; as he declared the imputation to be slanderous, a committee was appointed to investigate the matter, and report. "I was present," Mr. Baker says, "when, in the presence of two or three hundred citizens, the report was made, which affirmed that the charge against him was true! I saw the man the moment his character was thus blasted for ever. After one frantic effort, with a pistol, to take the life of the person who had thus exposed him, he dropped his head, and could not bear to look upon man or woman any more. Soon after returning to his lodgings, he laid himself down and died. Shame killed him!" How mysterious is the power of

SYMPATHY—which one describes as the natural check that the Almighty puts upon uncharitable self. In spite of themselves, there are few that have not felt compassion for others. This affords a beautiful proof both of the divine beneficence and of the power of the mind over the body. It is that inexplicable something in our moral and physical structure by which a multitude may be apparently possessed by the same spirit; the organism of each instantaneously taking on the same action, simply from the mind being devoted to the same object. There is no part nor organ of the body in which existing uneasiness may not be aggravated or relieved according as the attention is directed to the part or diverted from it. "Look at a person when yawning—read, or only think of it, and you begin to gape yourself. The wheezing and asthmatic struggles seen on one man, have been known to produce the same symptoms in another. Many obstinate and distressing coughs have been aggravated and prolonged by the mere apprehension of their return if relieved for a season." The physical effects of a

MORBID IMITATIVE SYMPATHY, and of IMAGI-

NATION, on the nervous system, are familiarly known. They have been displayed in all the various extravagancies which, at times, have attended the preaching of the gospel, and too often impeded its progress. The phenomena of this sort which are recorded in Dr. Davidson's "History of the Presbyterian Church in the State of Kentucky," are not less interesting to the psychologist and physician than they are to the preacher. They were occasioned, doubtless, in part, by an undue excitement of animal feeling. But the manifold forms, especially the "bodily exercises," by which this excited feeling was exhibited, have ever been, to some extent, inexplicable on any known principles of mental or physical science. They were classified under the significant names of the Falling, Rolling, Running, Dancing, Barking, and Jerking exercises, each of which was descriptive of a distinctive sort of bodily movement or agitation. We select, for an example, that muscular convulsion which was familiarly called the Jerks. The first recorded instance of its occurrence was at the administration of the Lord's

Supper in East Tennessee, when several hundred of both sexes were affected with this strange and involuntary contortion. "The subject was instantaneously seized with spasms or convulsions in every muscle, nerve, and tendon. His head was jerked or thrown from side to side with such rapidity that it was impossible to distinguish his visage, and the most lively fears were entertained lest he should dislocate his neck, or dash out his brains. His body partook of the same impulse, and was hurried on by like jerks over every obstacle—fallen trunks of trees, or, in a church, over pews and benches, apparently to the most imminent danger of being bruised and mangled. It was useless to attempt to hold or restrain him, and the paroxysm was permitted gradually to exhaust itself. An additional motive for leaving him to himself was the superstitious notion that all attempt at restraint was 'resisting the Spirit of God.' One remarkable feature of these bodily affections was, that the very apprehension of an attack would often bring it on in spite of all precaution or efforts of the will to prevent it.

A young man, the son of an elder, who was a tanner, feigned sickness on Sabbath morning to avoid accompanying the family to a camp-meeting. He was left alone in bed, with none in the house but a few black children. He lay some time triumphing in the success of his stratagem, but afraid to rise too soon, lest some one might be accidentally lingering, and detect him. As he lay quiet with his head covered, his thoughts were naturally directed to the camp-meeting, and fancy painted an assembled multitude, the public worship, and individuals falling into the usual spasmodic convulsions. All at once he found himself violently jerked out of bed, and dashed round the room and against the walls, in a manner altogether beyond his control. Recollecting that praying was said to be a good sedative on such occasions, he resorted to the experiment, and, to his great satisfaction, found it successful. He returned to bed quite relieved, but only to be again affected in the same way, and again quieted by the act of prayer. He then dressed himself, and to occupy his mind, went to the tanyard, and drawing a skin from the vat, prepared to take off the hair. He rolled up his sleeves, and grasping the knife, was about to commence operations, when instantaneously the knife was flirted out of his hand, and he himself jerked over logs, and against fences, as before. Gaining relief by resorting to the former remedy, he ventured to resume his occupation, and again was interrupted. But finding his talisman losing its efficacy, he began now to be really alarmed, and quitting the yard, he returned to his chamber and betook himself to prayer in good earnest. In this condition, weeping and crying to God for mercy, he was found by the family on their return. The result of this singular incident was, that he became a truly converted man, and shortly after connected himself with the church.

The same author mentions another example of the involuntary nature of these bodily exercises, in the case of a lady and gentleman of some note in the fashionable world, who were attracted to the camp-meeting at Cane Ridge by mere curiosity. On the way they amused themselves with a variety of jokes upon the poor deluded creatures who allowed themselves to roll screaming in the mud, and crying for mercy; and sportively agreed, that if either of them should fall, the other should remain, and render suitable protection and assistance. They had not been long on the ground, when, to the consternation of the gentleman, his gay companion suddenly dropped; whereupon, instead of fulfilling his promise, he fled at full speed. Flight, however, proved no preservative, for he had not gone two hundred yards before he was seized in the same way, and measured his own length upon the ground; while a crowd flocked around him to witness his mortification, and offer prayers in his behalf.

Very much like this, and equally marvellous, are the bodily exercises which have attended the late work of grace in Ireland. Dr. Macnaughton says, that "persons would be suddenly struck down as if they were dead; and not under the influence of exciting appeals made to them, for the same things happened to them when they were alone, and no person speaking to them."

Instructive exemplifications of our subject, concerning the power of the imagination, might be taken from the records of empiricism. Every feat of medical charlatanry has been a signal illustration of the strong reciprocal influence of the mind and the body. In the early part of the present century, a native of New England reaped a harvest of more than ten thousand pounds sterling from grateful, but deluded patients in Great Britain, whom he had relieved of distressing maladies by means of his "metallic tractors." These were two small pieces of metal of different kinds, which received their name from being drawn slightly over the part of the body affected, and which were said to attract the disease to the surface. That these marvellous cures were produced by the imagination of the sufferer, was proved by Dr. Haygarth, who had a couple of wooden tractors made, to resemble in appearance the metallic. The tractors of both sorts were afterwards applied to five patients, and the same benefit followed, whether the instrument used was made of wood or of iron; thus demonstrating the whole to be a grand imposture. It was a case which clearly belongs to the same category with that related of Dr. Woodhouse, who tested the power of imagination on certain persons, who, when nitrous oxide excited great attention, were anxious to breathe the gas. He administered to them ten gallons of atmospherical air, in doses of from four to six quarts. Impressed with the idea that they were inhaling the exhilarating gas, they soon began to exhibit the usual quickness of pulse, vertigo, ringing in the ears, difficulty of breathing, faintness, weakness of the knees, and nausea, which lasted from six to eight hours.

Bartholini, a famous physician, born at Copenhagen (1616,) declares that he once, by mistake, gave a patient a bottle of mere water instead of another bottle of liquor designed for an emetic, and that the patient's imagination was so affected by the expectation, that the water produced the effect he intended.

Franciscus Borri, born at Milan in the beginning of the seventeenth century, was said to cure all diseases, and so great was his reputation, that patients were carried to him from a great distance. But when it came to be observed that he cured only those who had a strong imagination, his credit sunk at once, and he worked no more wonders. A most remarkable example of the irresistible power of a disquieted mind is mentioned by Gregorius Leti, in his history of the Duke D'Ossuna. He tells us that a rich Neapolitan merchant, Jacob Morel, prided himself in not having once set his foot out of the city during forty-eight years. This coming to the ears of the Duke, Morel had notice sent to him that he was to take no journey out of the kingdom under the penalty of ten thousand crowns. The merchant smiled at receiving the order, but afterwards, not being able to fathom the reason of such a prohibition, grew so uneasy, that he paid the fine, and took a little trip out of the kingdom.

Selden, in his "Table-Talk," mentions the case of a gentleman that had been in a prolonged state of melancholy, whose malady I relieved, he says, by the following very simple expedient. "Perceiving his great confidence in me, and knowing that his complaint was rather fancied than real, I desired him to let me alone for a short time, and then come again, when I would give him directions, which, if faithfully followed, would cure him. In the meantime I got a card, and wrapped it in a handsome piece of taffeta, to which I put strings, and when he came, gave it to him to hang about his neck. At the same time I charged him not to disorder himself with improper eating and drinking; take very little supper, attend as usual to his devotional duties as he went to bed, and in a short time he would be well. Three or four days after, I called upon him, and found him very much better, but perceiving that there was still a remnant of his mental disquiet, I gave him another string to hang about his neck. Three days after, he came to my office in the Temple, and professed that he was as well as he had ever been in his life, and thanked me for the care I had taken of him. The gentleman lived many years, and was never troubled after."

Similar examples of the reflected influences of the mind and body on each other might be easily adduced to a much greater extent. We have indulged in our selections already to a profuseness perhaps, but the truths they illustrate cannot be presented in too many phases, nor too deeply impressed. It is a branch of the great subject of Moral Therapeutics, which is too little studied by those who are charged with the health of either the body or of the soul. They may be read with advantage by many, as interesting psychological facts, and at the same time help to prepare them for the more interesting part of our inquiry—the illustrations of this connection between the outer and inner man, as furnished by

III. CHRISTIAN EXPERIENCE.

We have already said, that it is a subject which is worthy the attention of all, whatever their character, moral or religious; but it is more particularly the case of the latter that this investigation contemplates. It is to show the influence of the mind and feelings upon the body, as well as the constant and yet often unsuspected actings of the flesh, with its unnumbered infirmities, upon the spirit; and that the devotional exercises of the latter are greatly affected by the physical condition of the former. And if the foregoing observations have been uninteresting, or unintelligible to any, there are those who will understand us now. Here we strike a chord which will vibrate more or less in every changed heart that has been given to the study of its own exercises. No person accustomed to notice his various religious frames, can have failed to perceive that these are closely allied to what is usually denominated his "constitution." Is there such a blending of the juices of the animal economy as to produce what is called a nervous temperament, or that excess of bile which makes it melancholy? Or is the man gentle or serene, sanguine or timid, cheerful or sad, you will find that these idiosyncrasies will not be merged and lost in the changes wrought by regenerating grace. His religion will not so neutralize and remove the cause of his lowness of spirits, his timidity, or whatever it may be that is peculiar to his nature, as to make him at all times cheerful and self-possessed. The bashful man will be a bashful Christian; and the bold man, constitutionally, will be bold in a state of grace. After all that the Spirit has accomplished in each, it will still be true in all, that the religious character will be tinctured by that of the natural man, as the liquor put into an old cask commonly receives a strong tang from the vessel.

> Quo semel est imbuta recens, servabit odorem
> Testa diu.
>
> The odours of the wine, that first shall stain
> The virgin vessel, it shall long retain.—FRANCIS.

In this respect the Spirit's operation on the soul has been happily compared to the work of a sculptor, who makes a statue of wood, of stone, or of marble, indifferently, according to the material put into his hand. So the

Spirit, in forming the new man, still retains so much of the old as to make it evident what is the rock from which he was hewn. Nor is it a less interesting fact, that this gracious influence is so exerted in the various conditions of life where it is felt, as to qualify the soul for the appropriate duties of its particular station. Does regenerating grace find a man in high life or humble, in Cæsar's household, among the fishermen of Galilee, or the servants of Philemon, it requires no change in his place, but works a change on his heart, and gives new help to discharge his duties better. The same Holy Spirit who makes a Christian master gentle and prudent in commanding, makes a Christian servant faithful and cheerful in obeying; as the astrologers said of Cyrus, that the same stars which made him to be chosen king amongst the armies of men when he came to be a man, made him to be chosen king among the shepherds' children when he was a child. In rearing the New Testament temple of the Redeemer on earth, there is the same occasion for various gifts and kinds of service that there was in the magnificent structure of Solomon. And hence the innocent and useful differences between men, in their fallen state, are preserved and turned to a profitable account in their recovery. See a familiar illustration of this in the original teachers of the gospel, or the twelve apostles. Simon Peter was by natural temperament ardent, sanguine, precipitate; and this characteristic of the natural man is continually betraying itself after his conversion. You observe it in his conversations with his Master; his bold professions, hasty promises, which opened the way for his sifting by Satan, and his lamentable fall. After the resurrection, see him running with John to visit the sepulchre; and while his timid and cautious companion stoops down at first, and only ventures to look into the place, the intrepid Peter rushes by and plunges into the gloomy abode of the dead, examines the very spot where the sacred dust had rested, and the linen clothes in which it had been wrapped. Both of them regenerated men, and men perhaps of equal piety; but very unlike before their conversion, and scarcely more alike afterwards. Dr. Mason used to say, that the grace which would make John appear like an angel, would be only just enough to keep Peter from knocking a man down.

Look next at Paul, whose lofty bearing, and undaunted courage by nature, was not a whit impaired, but only sanctified by grace, and retained to the end of his life. See Luther and Melancthon, as opposite in their Christian character as they were in their original temperament. "Melancthon," Cecil says, "is like a snail with his couple of horns; he puts out his horns and feels—and feels—and feels. No education could have rendered these two men alike. Their difference began in the womb. Luther dashes in saying his things; Melancthon must go round about." The same divine influence had wrought effectually on the heart of both; yet, like the statue of which we spoke, the image corresponded to the material out of which it had been constructed. That any amount of spiritual influence should ever destroy these physical characteristics and make men of such divers temperaments alike, is to be expected no more than that it should make them of one stature, or give them the same features or complexion.

It will be recollected how Cæsar recognizes the influence of temperament, when he objected to Cassius, because he was "lean and thought too much." He wished to have around him

> Sleek headed men, and such as sleep o' nights.
> Would he were fatter.

Such men as Cassius feared are usually "lean," because their "too much" thinking developes the brain and the nervous system at the expense of some function in the animal or organic. Men of this sort, according to Dr. Johnson, will be found thin and sallow, with weak digestion, and quickness or irritability of nerve, like Lord Wellington or Bonaparte, till the latter became bloated by disease. Martin Luther's amazing executive powers were as closely connected with his physical qualities as with his moral. His great mind was lodged in a body which seemed to have been created for just such a tenant. His frame was large, well proportioned, athletic, and capable of enduring, without fatigue, any amount of labour and privation. He was affable, hopeful, and a stranger to those bodily ailments that so beset and embitter the life of the sedentary and studious. Dr. Cox is reported to have said, that it was well that Luther was not a dyspeptic, for the Reformation would have been delayed, had he wanted a good digestion.

But there are other, and in some respects more marked and painful illustrations, in the morbid experience of some Christians, which are at once an effect and a symptom of the state of their health. Rev. Timothy Rogers, a minister in London near the close of the seventeenth century, who was happily delivered from long affliction and great spiritual distress produced by this cause, describes the condition as one which is in every respect sad and overwhelming. In a letter to a friend he says, "It is a state of darkness that has no discernible beams of light. It is a land of darkness, on which no sun at all seems to shine. It does generally, indeed, first begin at the body, and then conveys its venom to the mind; and if anything could be found that might keep the blood and spirits in their due temper and motion, this would obstruct its further progress, and in a great measure keep the soul clear." How many belong to that class who are familiarly said to look only at the dark side of every object, and are unwilling to engage in any enterprise, from an anticipation of its failure. Whether the happiness of this world or the next be their pursuit, the prospect is cheered by scarcely a ray of hope. Such a tendency to gloom is a *thorn in the flesh*, by which they are often tormented; nor is any class more exposed to the buffetings of this *minister of Satan*, than the teachers of religion. How often do we witness the sad spectacle of those whose manifold bodily infirmities, brought on by sedentary habits, great anxiety, or excessive study and exhaustion of sensorial power, defraud them of all the consolations of that benignant system of faith which they are enabled to expound so successfully to others. Instead of an open, cheerful expression of countenance, we often see a wrinkled, contracted, sinister look, which speaks anything but in favour of the benign religion of the gospel. Thus, Christianity itself is made to suffer from the physical sufferings of its professors and expounders. The light-minded and thoughtless imbibe a prejudice against it, from observing the care-worn and sorrowful features of some of its advocates. They think it to be a legitimate effect of their principles, and are made to shun the places, and books, and people, whose influence appears to be so detrimental to all earthly enjoyment. Unhappily, these outward tokens of disquietude are but too significant of what is passing within. If the face be covered with gloom, it is only an index of the state of such a Christian's heart, when in the retirement of his closet he pours out its exercises in lamentations, and confessions of sin, and supplications for relief. At one time, he feels that he has grieved the

Spirit, that his best services are only hypocritical forms, and surely *God has forsaken him.* His heart appears like the *nether millstone*, and his bosom *the cage of every unclean bird. The arrows of the Almighty are within him, the poison whereof drinketh up his spirit, and the terrors of God do set themselves in array against him.* Again the scene is wholly changed; the turbid current of his thoughts has become clear as crystal. *The rain is over and gone, and the time of the singing of birds is come.* The change in his exercises is like the transition from the terrific tempest to the serene sky, and air, and pleasant sun, that follow it. *Or ever he is aware, his soul makes him like the chariots of Amminadib.* His doubts are solved, his fears are gone, and his present joys perhaps are in proportion to his previous sadness. He is brought into Christ's *banqueting house, and the banner over him is love. He is stayed with flagons and comforted with apples,* and restored to the joys of salvation.

That such spiritual fluctuations as these, to which so many Christians are subject, are very often produced by physical causes, is as capable of proof, as it is that an excited pulse and increased heat are symptoms of fever. They are the reflected influence of some bodily malady upon the soul. They arise, as Rev. Dr. J. R. McDuff says, from a diseased body, an overstrung mind—a succession of calamities, weakening and impairing the nervous system. We know how susceptible are the body and mind together, of being affected by external influences. Of that constitution which, in our ignorance, we call union of soul and body, we know little respecting what is cause and what is effect. We would fain believe that the mind has power over the body; but it is just as true that the body rules the mind. Causes apparently the most trivial—a heated room, want of exercise, a sunless day, a northern aspect—will make all the difference between happiness and unhappiness; between faith and doubt; between courage and indecision. To our fancy there is something humiliating in being thus at the mercy of our animal organism. We would fain find nobler causes for our emotions. But many of those sighs and tears, and morbid, depressed feelings which Christians speak of as the result of spiritual darkness and the desertion of God, are merely the result of physical derangement; the penalty often for the violation of the laws of health. The atmosphere we breathe is enough to account for them. They come and go, rise and fall, with the mercury in the tube. These are cases not for the spiritual, but for the bodily physician. Their cure is in attendance to the usual laws and prescriptions which regulate the healthy action of the bodily functions. We once knew a man of superior natural gifts and piety, an officer of the church, who suffered occasionally from such a cause. The effect on his devotional feelings was so marked, that you could discover the state of his health in his prayers. They were always excellent and edifying, yet there was at times a subdued manner, or a sadness, which indicated the influence of bodily infirmity, and of the struggle of the soul to resist the tendency.

Many have discovered that their periods of

spiritual depression are always contemporaneous with periodical changes in their physical condition, or with that sort of indisposition which proceeds from gastric derangement or an affection of the liver. How many thousands are daily affected by changes in the atmosphere, scarcely less than was Dr. Francia, Dictator of Paraguay, whose most extravagant outbreaks of passion, and cruel exertions of despotic power, generally occurred during his seasons of hypochondria, which were most frequent when the wind was north-east, but which ended with a change to south-west, when he would begin to sing and laugh to himself, and was readily accessible. Sir Woodbine Parish informs us, in his narrative of a visit to Buenos Ayres, that a sort of moral derangement prevails when the wind blows from the north; that quarrels and bloodshed are much more frequent at such times than at any other. He relates that a gentleman of amiable manners under ordinary circumstances, was so affected by this wind, that whenever it prevailed, he would quarrel with any one he met; and he was at last executed for murder, after having been engaged in street-fights, with knives, at least twenty times.

The cases in which this sort of morbid suffering is exemplified are so numerous, that their *name is Legion.* They find that their state while here "is a conjunction of their soul to a frail distempered body, and so near a conjunction, that the actions of the soul must have great dependence on the body. Its apprehensions of spiritual good are limited by the frailty of the body, and the soul can go no higher than the body will allow." We have known instances in which the seasons of spiritual joy and depression alternated like an intermittent disease, coming and departing at regular intervals. In the church of the late Dr. Spencer, of Brooklyn, New York, was an excellent female, whose "mind was found to be shrouded in darkness and gloom. After many conversations held at different times for months, one day I called upon her," he says, "and to my surprise found her calm, and that her distress of spirit had given place to gladness. But three days after this, her light had departed and she had relapsed into her former state of despair. Not long after, she became hopeful and happy for a little season, and then as depressed and sorrowful as ever. These alternations from gloom to gladness were inexplicable, until I was able to connect them with the state of her bodily health. When I mentioned the cause to her, she admitted the coincidence between the coming of pain into her head and the departure of her spiritual peace; but this explanation seemed credible only during her intervals of peace, which at length became short. In the morning she was always hopeful, but every afternoon in despair. In the morning she believed that her afternoon distress was caused by her bodily infirmity, but would entirely disbelieve it in the afternoon. At length the morbid bodily state which had so affected her mind was changed. The light of Christian hope and joy were no longer withdrawn. Her death was peaceful, without a doubt of a happy immortality."

During Mr. Cecil's protracted sickness of

three years, the state of his mind fluctuated with his malady. Its principal effect was apparent in throwing a cloud over his comfort. He was precisely like a man laden with a heavy weight. As the load was lightened, he began to think, feel, exert and enjoy himself in his natural manner. When the burden was increased, he sank down again under the oppression. Sometimes these intermissions are much more prolonged, as in the case of the late excellent and venerable Dr. James Hall, of North Carolina, who was of a melancholy temperament; and after finishing his education at Princeton he fell into a gloomy dejection, which interrupted his studies and labours for more than a year. After his restoration he laboured successfully and comfortably in the ministry many years, even to old age; but at last was overtaken again, and entirely overwhelmed by this terrible malady. "Of all men that I ever saw," Dr. A. Alexander says, "he had the tenderest sympathy with persons labouring under religious despondency. When on a journey, I have known him to travel miles out of his way to converse with a sufferer of this kind; and his manner was most tender and affectionate in speaking to such."

A venerable clergyman, who had suffered greatly from nervous affections, discovered this to be characteristic of his own experience; that when the period of gloom and distress did not terminate for two or three weeks, it would in the meantime recur only every other day. But the more common cases are those in which the cloud, when gathered, remains suspended and unmoved for days or weeks, with scarcely a gleam of sunshine. Such a sufferer was the late eminently learned and pious Isaac Milner, Dean of Carlisle, whose extraordinary talents and attainments in science were conceded by all, and whose genuine piety was questioned by none but himself. And yet, while the source of so much light and spiritual instruction to others, he was often an opaque and cheerless body to himself. "Though I have endeavoured to discharge my duty as well as I could," he writes to Mr. Wilberforce, "yet sadness and melancholy of heart stick close by and increase upon me. I tell nobody, but I am very much sunk indeed, and I wish I could have the relief of weeping as I used to do." Again, in writing to another, a clerical friend, he says, "My views have of late been exceedingly dark and distressing; in a word, Almighty God seems to hide his face. I entrust the secret hardly to any earthly being. I know not what will become of me. There is doubtless a good deal of bodily affection mingled with this, but it is not all so. I bless God, however, that I never lose sight of the cross; and though I should die without seeing any personal interest in the Redeemer's merits, I think, I hope, that I should be found at his feet. I will thank you for a word at your leisure. My door is bolted at the time of my writing this, for I am full of tears." Such spiritual sadness is easily accounted for, when it is understood that Dr. Milner was for upwards of forty years a victim of some of the most distressing complaints that flesh is heir to. Spasms in his stomach, severe and uninterrupted headaches, oppression of the breath, broken slumbers, disturbed by frightful dreams, were among the diseases which caused his physicians to tell him, many years before his death, that with such a pulse as his, a man's life was not worth one minute.

Another example is furnished by Richard Baxter, in whose practical and devotional writings it is easy to discover the constitutional habits and qualities of the man. No person, not inspired, ever wrote more graphically of heaven and hell, as if he had visited both, and had come back to the earth again to exhort men to seek the one and escape the other. But, notwithstanding his pre-eminent piety, during his early years his mind was greatly troubled with doubts about his own salvation, promoted, says his biographer, by the particular cast of his mind, and the state of his body. And, though habitually under the government of religious principles, it is well known that he had certain besetting infirmities of temper, which are among the most common diagnostics of what were some of his manifold diseases. The late Dr. Payson was another, whose vibrations of Christian feeling, from the joyous to the sad, the cheerful to the desponding and melancholy, are scarcely less notorious than were his uncommon zeal and ministerial success. The cause is at once explained, when his biographer tells us that his physical conformation was of a very delicate structure, extremely sensitive, and easily excited, so that nervous irritability and consequent depression were an ingredient in his nature. Hence, he adds, we have seen him writing bitter things against himself, for causes which, with a different temperament, would have given him little uneasiness. The case of David Brainerd, the apostolic missionary, is in some respects more marked and instructive on this subject than even Payson's. But it is easy to make the almost opposite and contradictory details of his diary harmonize with one another, and both with eminent godliness, when the writer of his Memoirs, President Edwards, tells us of his frail health, and of his constitutional proneness to dejection and melancholy. His willing spirit would have made him a rival of Paul, but under the weakness of his flesh he sunk before he reached the age of thirty.

Such illustrations need not be multiplied, and yet we cannot forbear to advert, for a moment, before we pass on, to the touching case of one in whose character there is an abiding interest, which affords a guaranty that the repetition, even of that which is familiarly known, will not be tiresome. And perhaps within the range of casuistic research, we could not find a more affecting instance of morbid religious affection, than that of Cowper. How long his mind was shrouded in darkness, and racked with the most fearful forebodings, is as widely known as is his name. In one of his somewhat playful moods, when writing to the Rev. John Newton, "my thoughts," he says, "are clad in a sober livery, for the most part as grave as that of a bishop's servant. They turn, too, upon spiritual subjects; but the tallest fellow, and the loudest among them all, is he who is continually crying out with a loud voice, *actum est de te*, *periisti*—it is all over, you are lost." But what was the state of his mind for many years, is nowhere described in more affecting terms than in the last original poem which he ever wrote, and which he called the Castaway. It was founded on an incident mentioned in Lord Anson's Voyages, which he had read many years before, though the concluding stanzas show that the real subject of his muse was not the sufferer mentioned by Anson: for having described the case of the unhappy mariner, his being washed headlong from on board,

> Of friends, of hope, of all bereft;

his sinking beneath the "whelming brine;" then rising to the surface, struggling among the waves, his crying for help, the efforts made to save him, the mournful sound of his voice, heard in every blast by his comrades, as the ship was driven farther and farther from him, till they

> Could catch the sound no more;

when, overcome at length, and exhausted, he sunk; the poet then adds:

> I therefore purpose not, or dream,
> Descanting on his fate,

> To give the melancholy theme
> A more enduring date:
> But misery delights to trace
> Its semblance in another's case.
>
> No voice divine the storm allayed,
> No light propitious shone;
> When snatched from all effectual aid,
> We perish'd each alone;
> But I beneath a rougher sea,
> Am whelm'd in deeper gulfs than he.

That the cause of Cowper's spiritual depression was disease, has been abundantly proved to all, unless it be those "who would far sooner tolerate a poet's being a madman than his being a saint." His despondency was produced by physical causes, which could not be removed by reasoning, any more than a headache or a paroxysm of the gout. So the sufferer himself appears to believe, as is more than implied in the following extract from one of his letters:—"The mind of man is not a fountain, but a cistern, and mine, God knows, a broken one. Sally Perry's case has given us much concern; I have no doubt it is distemper. But distresses of mind that are occasioned by distemper are the most difficult of all to deal with. They refuse all consolation; they will hear no reason. God only, by his own immediate impressions, can relieve them, as after an experience of thirteen years' misery I can abundantly testify." Like other valetudinarians of a particular class, his nerves were as sensitive to atmospheric changes as is the mercury of the barometer. He was joyful or sad, as the day was serene or cloudy. "I rise cheerless or distressed," says he to one of his friends, "and brighten as the sun goes on." He had his four seasons of feeling, as the revolving earth described the four grand stages of the sun's progress in the ecliptic. Thus, in another of his letters, he says: "I now see a long winter before me, and am to get through it as I can. I know the ground before I tread upon it: it is hollow; it is agitated; it suffers shocks in every direction; it is like the soil of Calabria—all whirlpool and undulation. But I must reel through it; at least, if I be not swallowed up by the way."

In a brief notice of Cowper by Mr. Cecil,

he alludes to an "unfounded report" in circulation, that the poet's melancholy was derived from his residence and connection at Olney. The fact, however, Mr. Cecil says, was just the reverse, as was attested both by respectable living witnesses, and by manuscripts of Cowper's own writing at the calmest period of his life. Many years before, and shortly after he began the study of law, he had a fearful attack, which was alleviated by reading the Gothic and uncouth poems of pious George Herbert. This relief, however, was only for a season. His thoughts were constantly tending back towards the same turbid channel from which they had been diverted. Then again he would be tempted to all sorts of evil—to murmuring against Providence, scepticism, disgust of life, and even to suicide. And yet, whenever relief came, even for a season, it was attended with a renewed interest in the Bible, and a lively faith in its distinguishing doctrines. The longest and happiest period of his life was at St. Albans, under the care of Dr. Cotton, a physician as capable of administering to the spiritual as to the natural maladies of his patients. The vast black wall which he represented as visibly erected between himself and heaven, Dr. Moore says, was some impediment to the right action of his brain in relation to thought and sight. His disease was kept up by monotony and medicine. There were none but quackish attempts at cure, except while under the care of Dr. Cotton, who for a time relieved, and, had his advice been properly followed out, would have probably cured him. It was from his treatment that Cowper first obtained a clear view of those sublime and animating truths which so distinguished and exalted his future strains as a poet. Here also he received that settled tranquillity and peace, which he enjoyed for several years afterwards. So far, therefore, was his constitutional malady from being produced or increased by his evangelical connections, either at St. Albans or at Olney, that he seems never to have had any settled peace but from the truths learned in these societies. It appears that among them alone he found the only sunshine he ever enjoyed through "the cloudy day of his afflicted life." While residing with this excellent friend, his distress was for a long time entirely removed by the passage in Romans: *Him hath God set forth to be a propitiation, through faith in his blood, to declare his righteousness for the remission of sins that are past.* In this scripture he saw the remedy which God provides for the relief of a guilty conscience, with such clearness, that, for several years after, his heart was filled with love, and his life occupied with prayer, praise, and doing *good to all as he had opportunity.* Mr. Newton told me, Cecil says, that from Cowper's first coming to Olney, it was observed he had studied his Bible with such advantage, and was so well acquainted with its design, that not only his troubles were removed, but that to the end of his life he never had clearer views of the peculiar doctrines of the gospel than now when he first became an habitual hearer of them. That during this period the inseparable attendants of a lively faith appeared, by his exerting himself to the utmost of his power in every benevolent service he could render to his poor neighbours; and that Mr. Newton used to consider him as a sort of curate, from his constant attendance upon the sick and afflicted in that large and necessitous parish.

CHAPTER II.

USES OF KNOWLEDGE ON THIS SUBJECT.

I was a stricken deer, that left the herd
Long since. With many an arrow deep infixed
My panting sides were charged.—COWPER.

THOUGH the character of this discussion, as well as its limited scope, have precluded many important remarks which come within the province of the physiologist, yet much that might be written is rendered unnecessary, by a knowledge which many derive from their own experience. It is a subject which, as we have said before, is too little examined and understood. "Many of our young preachers," Dr. Alexander says, in his instructive book on Religious Experience, "when they go forth on their important errand, are poorly qualified to direct the doubting conscience, or to administer safe consolation to the troubled in spirit. And in modern preaching there is little account made of the various distressing cases of deep affliction under which many serious persons are suffering. To no small proportion of the religious, both teachers and people, it seems to be a profound secret, how much the exercises of a changed heart may be affected by the health or the condition of the body." They cannot understand how a man's brain and nervous system may so suffer from faults in his digestive organs, as to produce irritability of temper, unsteadiness in any pursuit or application, distrust of friends, fear of evil tidings, and doubts concerning his own salvation. These are commonly regarded as moral affections, whereas they are in reality physical evils, which are to be remedied or removed by physical means. They are as legitimately symptoms of disease as is nausea, dimness of vision, or headache. And is a man unable to judge himself, much less is he qualified to meet the numerous cases that are almost daily presented in an extensive pastoral charge, when unskilled to distinguish, with some degree of accuracy, between influences which proceed from the body, and the principles, disposition, and state of the soul. As a part of his furniture for some of the most responsible labours of his calling, he needs a thorough acquaintance with a subject so closely connected with Christian experience.

Among the counsellors who so much aided the Rev. Timothy Rogers in his period of spiritual darkness, he quotes old Mr. Greenham as saying "that there is a great deal of wisdom requisite to consider both the state of the body and of the soul. If a man that is troubled in conscience comes to a minister, it may be he will look all to the soul, and nothing to the body; if he cometh to a physician, he considereth the body, and neglecteth the soul. For my part, I would never have the physician's counsel despised, nor the labour of the minister neglected; because the soul and body dwelling together, it is convenient that as the soul should be cured by the word, by prayer, by fasting, or by comforting, so the body must be brought into some temperature by physic and diet, by harmless diversions, and such like ways—providing always, that it be so done in the fear of God, as not to think by these ordinary means quite to smother or evade our troubles, but to use them as preparatives, whereby our souls may be made more capable of the spiritual methods that are to follow afterwards."

The practical uses of the knowledge of which we come to speak now, cannot be fully enumerated, nor adequately described. As the apostle says of the inspired truth which he commends to Timothy, we would say, that it "is profitable for"

Doctrine.

We mean to say, that here is presented a theory in casuistic divinity which solves innumerable cases of constant occurrence, by which many are often confounded without it. It is admitted that there is a difficulty to be encountered, in turning such doctrine on the subject of our spiritual maladies to a beneficial result, on account of the inability to convince the sufferer of the real cause of his despondency. He seems to lack the capacity of perceiving, or of applying the sort of truth which his case requires, however plainly it may be set before him; for, as President Edwards observes, in speaking of Brainerd, it is rare that melancholy people are sensible of their own disease—and that such things are to be ascribed to it as are undoubtedly its genuine fruits or effects. Otherwise we should be amazed at the perplexity and disconsolateness of some excellent characters, and the readiness with which they refuse to be comforted. Even the acute and discriminating Dr. Rush, so skilful in explaining and relieving the maladies of others, was utterly deceived in relation to his own. His Essay on the Influence of Physical Causes upon the Moral Faculty, evinces mature reflection, and accurate knowledge on this subject; and yet, when, in a state of religious despondency himself, he was assured by his pastor that it was a symptom of disease, he could not believe it. Nor did he become fully convinced that the cause of his spiritual distress was physical,

9*

until it had been removed by the improvement of his general health. Indeed it is commonly found, that where mental depression results from impaired health, our attempts to relieve the mind by counsel tend rather to aggravate its sorrow, so long as the physical cause remains unmitigated. The Rev. Thomas Boston was, at one time, in such a state of doubt and spiritual depression during his ministry, without perceiving the cause, that he was tempted to give it up. But although this eminent Christian scholar was in so great darkness himself, he was a *burning and a shining light to others.* His exposition of Providence, under the quaint title of "Crook in the Lot," surpasses any work of the kind in our language. "I do not know that I could point out a work," Dr. A. Alexander says, "which is so well adapted to reconcile the afflicted saint to his lot in this world, and help him to improve the dealings of Providence towards him, especially in the 'dark and cloudy day' of adversity."

A late preacher, well known by his manifold

useful labours, writes in his diary:—"Many of my people, and especially females, talk thus to me—'I am under continual distress of mind; I can lay hold of no permanent ground of peace. If I seem to get a little, it is soon gone again. I am out at sea, without compass or anchor. My heart sinks, my spirit faints, my knees tremble; all is dark above, and all is horror beneath.' 'And pray, what is your mode of life?' 'I sit by myself.' 'In this small room, I suppose, and over your fire?' 'A considerable part of my time.' 'And what time do you go to bed?' 'I cannot retire till two or three o'clock in the morning.' 'And you lie late, I suppose, in the morning?' 'Frequently.' 'And pray what else can you expect from this mode of life than a relaxed and unstrung system, and, of course, a mind enfeebled, anxious, and disordered? I understand your case; God seems to have qualified me to understand it, by special dispensations. My natural disposition is gay, volatile, spirited. My nature would never sink. But I have sometimes felt my spirit absorbed in horrible apprehensions, without any assignable natural cause. Perhaps it was necessary I should be suffered to feel this, that I might feel for others; for certainly no man can have any adequate sympathy with others, who has never thus suffered himself. I can feel for you, therefore, while I tell you that I think the affair with you is chiefly physical. I myself have brought on the same feelings by the same means. I have sat in my study till I have persuaded myself that the ceiling was too low to suffer me to stand and rise upright, and air and exercise alone could remove the impression from my mind.'"

In the last illness of the commentator Scott, his mind was observed by his friends to be gloomy during the paroxysm of his fever; nor could his comfort be restored by any counsel of his pious attendants, until the fever had abated. Andrew Fuller also suffered greatly on his deathbed, from a similar cause. So when Dr. Madan once attempted to calm the mind of Cowper, by quotations from the Scriptures, it served only to increase his sufferings.

It was then at the commencement of a slow nervous fever, to which he was liable; but after four months skilful treatment by Dr. Cotton, his health was so far improved that the promises of the gospel were apprehended without hesitation, and whatever his friend Madan had said to him long before, revived in all its clearness. An aged minister of the gospel says, we have known persons, who were *poor in spirit, hungering and thirsting after righteousness, glorying only in the cross of Christ*, and yet gloomily concluding that they have no lot nor part in the matter, and that their *heart is not right* with God. And why? The reason is to be found in something beyond the preacher's province; and till there is a change in the animal economy, all the succours of religion are in vain.

In an admirable review of a paper on Moral Causes of Disease, by the Secretary of the Royal Academy of Medicine in Paris, the author reproaches his medical brethren for their ignorance or neglect. He chides them for the overlooking of psychological causes of disease, and of the influence of mental emotions on its development, its progress, and its termination. "If a patient dies," he says, "we open his body, rummage the viscera, and scrutinize most narrowly all the organs and tissues, in the hope of discovering lesions of some one sort or another. There is not a small membrane, cavity, nor follicle, which is not carefully examined. One thing only escapes our attention, which is this—we are looking at merely organic effects, forgetting all the while that we must mount higher up, to discover their causes. These organic alterations are observed, perhaps, in the body of a person who has suffered deeply from mental distress and anxiety, which have been the energetic cause of his decay; but they cannot be studied in the laboratory, nor in the amphitheatre." Another profitable use of this subject is, for the promotion of

CHARITY.

So far as it is understood and practically felt, it will make us pause before we censure those of our brethren whose condition rather claims our condolence and hearty commiseration. We think them morose, hypochondriac, or misanthropic; assail them with raillery and banter, and anon with reproof for feelings of sadness, which they can no more resist nor control, than they can prevent a flushed cheek in fever, or a yellow skin in jaundice. We might as well jeer at Dr. Watts for his pigmy size, at Pope for his deformity, or at Milton for his blindness. Dr. John Cheyne says, that of all the miseries which afflict human life, or relate principally to the body in this valley of tears, I think "nervous disorders, in their extreme and last degree," are the most deplorable, and beyond all comparison the worst. And yet there are many in society, even among the intelligent, who are accustomed to treat all such cases of nervous disorder, as only imaginary complaints, which are better managed by ridicule than by sober counsel, whether medical or religious. In order to cure them, they think it necessary only to divert the attention of the sufferer, and convince him that he will be well enough and recover his lost cheerfulness, if he will but cease to brood over his own wretchedness, mix in society, and think of other things beside himself. "Many will say to such an one, 'Why do you so pore over your case, and thus gratify the devil?' Whereas it is the very nature of the disease to cause such fixed musing. You might as well say to a man in a fever, 'Why are you not well? why will you be sick?' Some, indeed, suppose that the melancholy hug their disease and are unwilling to give it up. You might as well suppose that a man would be pleased with lying on a bed of thorns." The reason of their utter misapprehension of such cases, is their own happy exemption from all that sort of morbid wretchedness which they treat with so much levity in others, without knowing what they do. To persons of this description, moreover, all our disquisitions on the moral effect of physical causes, are much like a treatise in Tamul or Hindostanee: they have no just conception of our meaning, nor of the utility of what we say. Nor is it among the lighter afflictions of the subjects of nervous affections, that they receive so little charity or sympathy from others whose general intelligence, and especially religious pretensions, would warrant them to expect more courtesy at least, if not greater tenderness. "It is a foolish course which some take with their melancholy friends, to answer all their complaints and moans with this—that it is nothing but fancy; nothing but imagination and whimsey. It is a real disease, a real misery, that they are tormented with; and if it be a fancy, yet a diseased fancy is as great a disease as any other; it fills them with anguish and tribulation. But this so disordered fancy is the consequent of a greater evil, and one of the sad effects that are produced by that black humour that has vitiated all the natural spirits. These afflicted persons can never possibly believe that you pity them, or that you are heartily concerned for them, if you do not credit what they say; and truly it often falls out, that because melancholy persons do not always look very ill, or have pretty good stomachs, and do not at first very much decline in their bodies, other persons, that know nothing of the distemper, are apt to think that they make themselves worse than they are." But if our subject is unintelligible to some, it is not so to others; we describe an experience with which they are wofully familiar; and while they are not slow to condemn themselves for their fretfulness, irritability of temper, and many obliquities of feeling and conduct which they so frequently betray, yet their faults, however numerous, will be judged with least severity by those who best understand the cause. With nerves so disordered and unstrung, there is need of far more vigilance and prayer, to even appear cheerful and amiable, than most good men, without very special grace, are able to maintain. "A man may be a good performer, but what can he do with a disordered instrument? The occupant of a house may have good eyes, but how can he see accurately through a soiled window? Let the organ be put in tune, and the glass be made clean; before you call in question the musical skill of the one, or the eyesight of the other." Harsh speeches may fret, perplex, and enrage, but will never do the sufferers any good. In his excellent counsels on the subject of spiritual depression, Mr. Rogers says:—"Some indeed will advise you to chide and rebuke them upon all occasions; but I dare confidently say, such advisers never felt this disease; for if they had, they would know that by such a method they do but pour oil into the flame, and chafe and exasperate their wounds instead of healing them. Mr. Dod, by reason of his mild, meek, and merciful spirit, was reckoned one of the fittest persons to deal with people thus afflicted. Never was any minister more tender and compassionate. If you would be serviceable to such persons, you must not vex them with tart and rigorous discourse. It causes many poor souls to cherish and conceal their troubles, to their greater torment, because they meet with so very harsh entertainment from those to whom they have begun to explain their case. Our blessed Lord and principal Physician, was meek and lowly, and would not *break the bruised reed, nor quench the smoking flax.* And the first visit that the forementioned Mr. Dod made to Mr. Peacock in his anguish, was to put him in mind of God's kindness.

> Sunt verba et voces, quibus hunc lenire dolorem
> Passis, et magnam morbi deponere partem.—HOR. EPIST.
>
> The power of words and soothing sounds can ease
> The raging pain and lessen the disease.—FRANCIS.

Another most important use of this subject is for

REPROOF AND CORRECTION.

When thoroughly examined and well understood, it exposes and explodes the popular error in relation to those disordered states of the mind that are supposed by many to be produced by religion. Such events are deplorable whenever they occur, and whatever the occasion; but it would certainly be a remarkable exception to the general doctrines of philosophy as well as of religion, if it could be proved that these are the legitimate effect of so pure and benignant a cause. "This one thing I must testify," Dr. Alexander says, "that I never knew the most pungent convictions of sin to terminate in insanity; and as to the affections of love to God and the lively hope of everlasting life producing insanity, it is too absurd for any one to believe it." We readily concede that this belongs to a legion of evils, intellectual and moral, as well as physical, which are the natural product of fanaticism and superstition; and this explains the fact, that before the revolution so large a proportion of the insane in France were monks. Indeed, it is difficult to account for many of the effects of enthusiasm in any other way, than by supposing it to be a species of insanity in which the aberration relates usually to one subject, while in others the judgment is sound. And it is perfectly obvious, that the greatly multiplied cases of this kind of mental disorder at the present time, in different parts of our country, are the offspring of certain epidemical delusions by which we have been sorely afflicted of late, and which have been promoted by nothing so much as by the notice of others, and especially their attempts to suppress them by coercion. But we are sustained, not by the highest medical authority only, but by a faithful examination of the statistics of insanity, when we assert that the hallucinations of those persons whose mental disorder is imputed to religion, "are the result of pre-existing disease, and only take their form from the accidental habits and feelings of the patients." This has been so fully demonstrated, that scarcely any modern writer of eminence advocates the opposite opinion. From the numerous authors whose testimony is easily accessible, we will quote a paragraph from two or three, who are in the highest repute.

Dr. George Moore, member of the Royal College of Physicians, London, says: "That bodily disorder which favours the manifestation of the mind in an insane manner, may be produced by any of our passions when unrestrained by a holy understanding. The best blessings may thus be converted into curses; the best gifts into the most injurious agents. Some say religion is a frequent cause of insanity. No; true religion is the spirit of love, of power, and of a sound mind; ever active in diversified duties and delights; always busy in a becoming manner, and in decent order. But the wild notions, unmeaning superstitions, spiritual bondage, unrequired and forbidden attempts to reconcile the rites and ceremonies which wayward men have substituted for the liberty of God, begin in disobedience and end in darkness. It is *strange fire* in the censer which brings down the flaming vengeance, and opens a passage to the infinite abyss."

Of those subjects of what is called religious melancholy, or religious madness, who come under medical treatment, Dr. Ashbel Green says: "It is undeniable that the greater part are such as would previously be termed irreligious persons. Their religious anxiety has commenced with their mental aberration, and has disappeared on the restoration of health. In such cases, though the apprehension of divine anger may not seem unreasonable, it is as really an illusion as if the despondency had assumed the most alarming type. In fact, where religious anxiety or excitement has any share in producing mental aberration, this will generally put on the form of irreligious profaneness, or something contradictory of the previous healthful state of mind."

In regard to what are called the moral causes of insanity, Dr. Abercrombie says: "I suspect there has been a good deal of fallacy, arising from considering as a moral cause, that which was really a part of the disease. This, I think, applies in a peculiar manner to the important subject of religion, which by a common but very loose method of speaking, is often mentioned as a cause of insanity. But where there is a constitutional tendency to insanity, or to melancholy, one of its leading modifications, every subject is distorted to which the mind can be directed; and none more frequently or more remarkably, than religious belief. This, however, is the effect, not the cause; and the various forms which it assumes may be ascribed to the subject being one to which the minds of all men are so naturally directed in one degree or another, and of which no man living can divest himself."

Dr. Burrowes asserts, in his well known work on insanity, "that there is not a tittle of evidence to substantiate that Christianity, abstractedly, ever made a person insane. Such an accusation is only one of the abortions of infidelity, or of those who lack knowledge."

In Dr. Cheyne's interesting work on partial derangement of mind in supposed connection with religion, he says: "I never saw a case of mental derangement, even where it was traceable to a moral cause, in which there was not reason to believe that bodily disease could have been detected before the earliest aberration, had an opportunity of examination been offered. Not only does every deranged state of the intellectual faculties and the natural affections depend upon bodily disease, but derangements of the religious and moral sentiments also."

And, not to multiply authorities, we will add no more than a paragraph from Dr. Combe, who, in full concurrence with the others, maintains that "when fairly examined, the danger is seen to arise solely from the abuse of religion; and indeed, that the best safeguard is found in a right understanding of its principles and submission to its precepts. For if the best Christian be he who, in meekness, humility, and sincerity, places his trust in God, and seeks to fulfil all his commandments, then he who exhausts his soul in devotion, and at the same time finds no leisure or no inclination for attending to the common duties of his station, and who, so far from arriving at happiness or peace of mind, becomes every day the more estranged from them, and finds himself at last involved in disease and despair, cannot be held as a follower of Christ, but must rather be held as the follower of a phantom assuming the aspect of religion. When insanity attacks the latter, it is obviously not religion that is the cause; it is only the abuse of certain feelings, the regulated activity of which is necessary to the right exercise of religion; and against such abuse, a sense of true religion would have been the most powerful protection."

Dr. James Johnson contends that in every

case where the mind is said to be diseased, it ought to be considered as only a figure of rhetoric; that mind is merely an invisible agent, manifesting itself solely through the medium of the corporeal organs. When these last are deranged, the mental manifestations must also be deranged; but the mind itself remains unchanged, unassailable, imperishable. Even in insanity, it is not the mind which is diseased. Some portion of the brain is deranged, and then the mind can no more manifest itself sanely, than a musician can bring forth harmonious notes from an untuned instrument. As the mind is not material, neither is it liable to disease or death. If we once admit that it is subject to the one, we must inevitably come to the conclusion that it is liable to the other! With the essence or nature of mind, we are, and ever shall be ignorant. It is with the corporeal organs, through which it reveals its actions, that we have to do. If these have come into an abnormal or sickly condition, the effect will be often visible in the corresponding state of the intellect:

and if, at such a time, they be specially conversant with the subject of morals and religion, like a jaundiced eye, it will impart its morbid hue to them both.

The error of hastily ascribing religious melancholy to the direct agency or influence of religion, is exposed in the account given of a patient in the Pennsylvania Hospital in 1842, by Dr. Kirkbride, Physician to the institution.

"A young man of very moderate mental capacity, little education, and accustomed to a laborious occupation, from too much confinement at his business finds his health failing, and gives up his employment for a few months, to recruit. At the end of that time, although not well, he is able to return to work, but then discovers that the changes in the times make it impossible for him to find anything to do. His means being exhausted, his body weak, without his customary exercise, his mind gradually becomes in a morbid state, when some excitement from Miller's prophecy occurring in his neighbourhood, he immediately attempts to study the subject, and to ascertain its truth from close reading of the Bible—an investigation utterly unsuited for his capacity under any circumstances—and the difficulties he encounters at the very threshhold, lead to a violent attack of mania. The disease was attributed to 'Miller's prophecy,' or to 'religious excitement,' but neither of these causes would give a proper idea of the origin of the case. Before being excited on that subject, the patient's mind was ready to be overturned by any abstruse or exciting matter that might be presented to it. Without his loss of employment this would not have occurred, and without the enfeebled health which accompanied it, his attempted investigation might have been harmless."

Within the sphere of our own pastoral labours, there have occurred four cases of this species of mental disorder, three of which were connected with known physical derangement. Two were effectually relieved, after a few months, by judicious medical treatment, though one of them was so aggravated that the person attempted suicide, and on one occasion nearly effected it; the third still lingers, the sufferer being a victim of bodily disease. In the fourth there was a constitutional wildness on other subjects than that of religion; and although his temperament was sanguine, his mind habitually cheerful, and his hope of salvation uncommonly firm, yet in a moment of temptation he was overcome, and destroyed himself. Another, whom we have known for twenty years, and esteemed as a man of more than ordinary intellect and piety, has long been subject to periods of religious melancholy, when he suspends his business, loses all interest in society, withdraws to his chamber, and remains for weeks and months, until the cloud of spiritual gloom has passed; he then returns to his secular duties and to the church, as if he had never been otherwise than cheerful and happy in his religion, which is at all times, in sickness or health, his main topic of conversation. No allusion is made to the past, there are no inquiries, and he volunteers to give no information; nor have his friends or physicians ever been able to explain all the phenomena of this case by any of the known doctrines of psychology, physiology, or religion. That his melancholy is not produced by his religion, would appear from the fact, that at all other times it is the source of his highest enjoyment. But as it regards the cause of these periodical changes in his physical condition which occasion this spiritual occultation, we do not hazard a conjecture.

Not less injurious is the mistake of imputing to satanic agency what is dependent on bodily disease, as is exhibited in the case of the wife of the Rev. John Newton, who was unable to leave the house for nearly two years before she died, in 1790. In the beginning of October, she was confined to her bed, and was soon after deprived of all locomotive power. In this state, distress arose in her mind, which applied to the whole system of truth, and she said, "If there be a Saviour," "If there be a God;" and in this condition continued for a fortnight, when there is reason to believe that her doubts were removed. Mr. Newton accounted for his wife's temporary unbelief, by referring it to the influence of Satan. Mrs. Newton's, however, was a case of palsy—depending, as was supposed, upon a disease of the brain, by which her faith, the foundation of her religion, was disturbed, while her affections were uninjured. It is well known that Bunyan was grievously harassed at times with what he believed to be satanic temptations to the worst species of evil; and that Luther also supposed himself, on one occasion at least, to have been assaulted by the devil. But with regard to certain phenomena which it is common to refer to his influence, such as "unbidden and repulsive thoughts and feelings, and false perceptions, both voices and visions, that they *may* be produced by mere morbid physical agency, is unquestionable; because they are frequent accompaniments of pure disease, and yield with the disease, to medical treatment. Those, therefore, who are called to counsel persons thus afflicted, should never lose sight of the inquiry, whether such may not be the actual origin of what otherwise might be treated as temptations of the devil. That

Satan may have the power of injecting his malicious or blasphemous suggestions immediately into the mind, we have not intended at all to controvert. But we are disposed to adopt the principle of Dr. Cheyne, that, 'if an appeal to Him who conquered Satan, and who will aid all who come to him in faith, fails to relieve those who are thus afflicted, they may rest assured, that disease, and not the devil, is the enemy with which they have to contend,' and they must seek relief accordingly.

"And if we are pressed beyond this point with the hypothesis, that while disease may be the proximate cause of these distressing and horrible calamities, yet Satan may be the agent who employs this instrumentality to harass the Christian, we should be inclined to fall back upon the ground thus quaintly maintained by Richard Baxter: 'If it were, as some fancy, a possession of the devil, it is possible that physic might cast him out. For if you cure the melancholy, (black bile,) his bed is taken away, and the advantage gone by which he worketh;

cure the choler (bile) and the choleric operations of the devil will cease: it is by means and humours in us, that he worketh.'"

But this injurious influence on the mind has been ascribed, not so much to religion in general, as to certain forms or sectarian modes in which it has been expounded, and that are supposed to be peculiarly adapted to fill the soul with gloom and despondency. Hence the maxim, so long in vogue among the Romanists, "Spiritus Calvinianus, est spiritus melancholicus," (so nearly English that we need not translate it.) Even Esquirol more than hints at Calvinism as, in some cases, the cause of religious melancholy; and it is well known that the sentiment wrapped up in this calumnious apothegm was a popular solution of the unhappy case of Cowper. Thus, a writer in the Encyclopedia Britannica at that time, with great confidence ascribed his mental malady to the theory of justification which he had adopted, his natural disposition fitting him to receive all the horrors, without the consolations of his faith. Macaulay also favours the same opinion, by pronouncing the religious teachers of the poet "worthy of incineration." Nor is there anything, we are constrained to say, in the over cautious, imperfect, and disingenuous, however interesting Memoirs by Haley, that forbids this inference. And yet, it could not but have been known by the author, or rather compiler of that work, that the period of his life, during which he enjoyed, together with the unclouded sunshine of reason, the peace and joy of religion, was the interval from 1764 to 1773, when he believed and openly professed every article of his faith, the effect of which was represented as afterward being so calamitous. It was then that his character was exhibited in all its attractiveness, unveiled by any of the mists that had come over it before, and which gathered again toward the close of his life. He was more cheerful and affectionate in his intercourse, partaking with lively interest in the common concerns of society, and happy in the enjoyment of his religion; and when he became subsequently the victim of his afflictive hallucination, he could not avoid acknowledging that his gloomy persuasion was at variance with every article of his creed, and he was driven to regard himself as an inexplicable exception to his own principles. We have shown already that religious truth of any kind had nothing to do as a procuring cause of Cowper's malady. It was as clearly a case of hypochondriasis as are those instances in which the patient has fancied himself a tea-pot or a sack of wool; or as was that of the baker of Ferrara, mentioned by an Italian Count, who thought himself a lump of butter, and durst not sit in the sun, nor come near the fire, for fear of being melted, and his thinking substance destroyed.

We maintain then, that this unhappy condition, which, without due examination, has been imputed to religion, is an effect produced by physical causes. That a different opinion should have obtained to any extent, is to be ascribed to misapprehension, perhaps in part, but we doubt not that more frequently it may be traced to another source, which is thus noticed by Dr. Cheyne. "When a man from having been worldly becomes religious, there is no one against whom prejudice is stronger. No change is less agreeable, not even a change from respectability of conduct to the sort of profligacy which defies public opinion, than that which leads a man, whose previous motives were of a purely secular kind, to make the attainment of the kingdom of God his first object, by which he necessarily rises in the moral scale. That any one formerly on our own level should take, or affect to take higher ground, offends our self-love. It is a constant rebuke, by reminding us of his superiority of principle. Hence, it frequently happens that when a man really turns to God, first he is represented as a hypocrite, then a fool, and last of all, a madman. That his motives and his judgment will be arraigned, every neophyte may expect, as being matter of uniform experience; and that madness is a consequence of divine teaching, is a conclusion which is as old as the days of Portius Festus."

A well known minister of London, who has lately died, was called to visit a woman whose mind was disordered, and on remarking that it was a case which required the assistance of a physician rather than that of a clergyman, her husband replied, "Sir, we sent to you because it is a religious case; her mind has been injured by constantly reading the Bible." "I have known many instances," I replied, "of persons being brought to their senses by reading the Bible; but it is possible that too intense an application to that, as well as to any other subject, may have disordered your wife." "There is every proof of it," said he; and was proceeding to multiply his proofs, till her brother interrupted him by thus addressing me:—"Sir, I have no longer patience to stand by, and see you imposed on. The truth of the matter is this: my brother has forsaken his wife, and been long connected with an immoral woman. He had the best of wives in her, and one who was strongly attached to him; but she has seen his heart and property given to another, and, in her solitude and distress, went to the Bible as the only consolation left her. Her health and spirits at length sunk under her troubles; and there she lies distracted—not from reading her Bible—but from the infidelity and cruelty of her husband." The reader need not be told that the miscreant made no reply to his brother's statement, but immediately left the room in the utmost confusion. Another use of this subject, and the last which we shall mention, is for

CONSOLATION.

And for this grateful ministry, its scope is as wide as the office is benignant. As may be well presumed, this doctrine of physical influences is easily capable of being perverted. Some may mistake the buoyancy of animal spirits for the influences of the Comforter, and others may ascribe the *motions of sins which are by the law*, to the power of bodily disease. But it is not intended by this admission of the effect of physical causes upon the soul, to offer an apology for sin, to furnish a convenient excuse for indolence, sullenness, a cynical temper, or any other culpable dispositions to which a man may be constitutionally prone.

All these may be natural, but very criminal nevertheless. The difference is wide between a neglect of prayer and watchfulness occasioned by great fatigue in the performance of other duties, as in the case of the disciples in the garden, and an omission caused by giving way to an inbred laziness. As a question in morals, the point is material whether a man's hastiness of spirit be a symptom of hepatic disease, or the habitual prompting of a depraved and neglected heart. We are not accountable to God for the difference in our complexion, or in the length of our limbs, but he justly makes us responsible for the envy and jealousy and malice of our dispositions. Nor is it enough to refer such perplexing cases to the tribunal of conscience, in view of the well known influence of various moral, as well as physical causes, in misguiding its decisions. Not long ago we received, in a letter, the account of a young man of fervent piety, who was at this time preparing for the ministry; but in such a state, as to be wholly unable to pursue his studies. For several years he has felt himself urged and almost coerced, as he says, to make various vows to God, promising to spend so many hours a day in devotional exercises, and to keep days of fasting and prayer on various accounts. These vows have become so burdensome, as to interfere with his duty as well as with his peace. He has forgotten some of the reasons for these vows, and now he feels himself solemnly bound by his vow, but knows not what to do to fulfil it; and some of the occasions on which days of fasting were vowed to be kept, have passed, and his vow not fulfilled. He is kept awake a great part of the night, and is incapable of study. "I endeavoured," says my informant, "to show him, in what cases vows were not binding, and flattered myself that I had relieved his mind, but in a few days he came back, and I went over the whole again; but all to little purpose. And by this it may be commonly known, that the disease is physical, when the clearest reasoning and admitted conclusions produce no effect."

"Some time since," says the same correspondent, "I was consulted respecting the case of a young man, who, in obedience to his conscience, had vowed that he would never taste butter—but as this entered into so many kinds of food, he was kept in continual perplexity. This, however, seems to have been merely a device of Satan."

"Not long ago there was a pious and useful pastor in the interior of Pennsylvania, who, when pursuing his theological studies, resolved or vowed, against so many kinds of food, because they were gratifying to his palate, that he actually was suffering for want of nutritive food."

To what extent such religious whims, or any morbid exercises of persons in such an unhealthy mental condition are culpable, is perhaps the most perplexing inquiry which this whole subject suggests. That man is answerable for his conduct so long as "exaggerated irritability stops shorts of derangement," would seem to be an axiom in morals; and yet what shall we understand by derangement? What is that changed condition of the man, or how far must it go, in order to release him for the time, from the claims of the moral law? It has been confidently asserted, that the feelings produced by nervous diseases are not strictly moral, nor are we accountable for them except as we are accountable for inducing that state of physical organization in which they originate.

And admitting this also to be true, those cases will nevertheless continually occur which it will occasion no little perplexity to decide. Moral qualities, such as pride, envy, jealousy, covetousness, &c., we know are hereditary, as well as those that are intellectual: "Hence we often find," Dr. Rush says, "certain virtues and vices as peculiar to families through all their degrees of consanguinity and duration, as is a peculiarity of voice, complexion, or shape." But however this innate or transmitted tendency to certain kinds of evil may excite commiseration, we regard it not so much as an apology for having yielded to the inclination, as a cogent motive for continual vigilance against it. But notwithstanding the difficulties with which the subject is embarrassed, there is nevertheless, much in this doctrine of physical influences for the comfort of those whose wretched experience often makes it so desirable. It is a relief to find that they were in error concerning the nature of their distressing affection; to discover that what was supposed to be an infusion of Satan, has been caused, perhaps, by a mistake in the quality or quantity of their food, or by changes in the atmosphere. They see the danger of making their feelings the test of their Christian character, so long as their health is impaired. Indeed it is painful to read the diaries of many eminent believers, and see how they suffered from the imaginary belief of the withdrawment of God's favour, manifested, as they supposed, by the variable state of their feelings. Who but the victim himself can conceive of the wretchedness of a soul that vents its anguish in language such as the following: "I taste nothing but gall and wormwood; nothing but misery and vexation. *I was at ease, but he hath broken me asunder; he hath taken me by my neck and shaken me to pieces, and set me up for his mark; his archers compass me round about; he cleaveth my reins asunder, and doth not spare; he poureth out my gall upon the ground.* I dare not look up to heaven, for there I see how great a God I have against me; I dare not look into his word, for there I see all his threats as so many barbed arrows to strike me to the heart; I dare not look into the grave, because thence I am like to have a doleful resurrection. The Almighty is my enemy. The prayers of others can do me no good unless I have faith, and I find I have none at all, for that would purify and cleanse my heart. I do nothing else but sin; and God, as he is holy, must set himself against me, his enemy." The grand difficulty in many of these cases, lies in a deranged condition of the animal part. A highly respectable clergyman, still living in New England, after having preached with much acceptance and success to a congregation for twenty years, was called to another field of labour; the change proving not so happy in all respects as he had anticipated, his health failed, and with it his hope. On entering the pulpit one Sabbath morning, he sat for a while, then arose, and instead of commencing as usual the exercises of the day, he remarked to the people that he had been deceived in relation to his personal religion, was not worthy of the office of a preacher, and could not any longer discharge it. A physician who was present called on him afterwards, and was enabled to convince him that the cause of his despondency was physical. In the course of two weeks of medical treatment it was removed, his Christian hope revived, he resumed his labours as a preacher, and has continued to perform them ever since with comfort to himself and usefulness to others.

So far therefore, as it may be shown to the spiritually depressed that their gloominess is a symptom of disease, they may be consoled by the assurance, that such distress of their soul is perfectly consistent with its regenerate state and its safety. That the highest medical authority teaches, that whenever a change in the temper or mind takes place, without a plain and manifest moral cause, the condition of the liver or digestive organs should be examined; "for there will be found the origin of the mischief, three times out of four." Let them resort then to such remedies as the exigencies of the case demand, and wait for relief to be afforded through the proper channel.

The same consideration, moreover, may often minister substantial consolation in the case of departed friends, whose exercises have appeared more or less ambiguous, as flesh and heart were failing under the power of disease.

It is an important observation of Pearson, in his life of Mr. Hay, of Leeds, that good men may be unreasonably depressed, and bad men elevated, under the near prospect of death, from the mere operation of natural causes. The Saviour's declaration makes it fearfully certain that the judgment-day will reveal many disappointments of some rejected, who died in the confident hope of salvation; of others received, who left this world in darkness and despair. How difficult as well as delicate then, is the task of those who undertake to compile the memoirs of the pious from their diaries, or the records of their secret experience! How great their need of judgment, sound discretion, and especially of that knowledge of mental disorders and morbid influences, which many of such writers have evidently lacked! Indeed we are by no means convinced that there is not virtually a breach of trust in exposing the records of Christian experience, perhaps meant to be secret, to the inspection of the public. Such relations, moreover, while they have not benefitted the pious, have been subjects of merriment to the profane.

That the deeply interesting biography of Payson would have been more valuable by some omissions, will hardly be questioned by those who regard the portions to which we refer, as indicative rather of the state of his health than of the condition of his soul. And so of the amiable poet of Olney, who, through the whole period of his gloomy aberrations, kept a journal of his feelings, which was published after his decease, in spite of the earnest expostulations of his more judicious friends. It was regarded by them as a heartless violation of the secrets of the sepulchre, as a throwing open of the closet of the anatomist to the gaze of the vulgar, and a yielding to the pryings of a prurient curiosity, under a pretence of correcting certain false notions of religion.

How few of us would be willing to submit it to the most discreet friend that might survive us, to draw our religious character from what we might write from day to day of our religious exercises, under a full conviction at the time we penned it, of its truth! We say then, in conclusion, that while this doctrine is never to be used as an excuse for wilful delinquency in any, it may afford effective consolation to the afflicted believer when bowed down with infirmities of soul which he cannot overcome. If rightly understood it will tend not only to minister relief, but will make us more watchful against sin in all its forms, and especially against that to which we have a constitutional bias. Are we naturally passionate and excitable; are we envious, proud, covetous, or jealous, it will cause us to pray and watch against these besetting sins with peculiar vigilance; while our numerous failures in this and every other duty, will make us feel our absolute dependence on the Spirit, both for grace to enjoy our religion, and strength to obey its precepts. Above all, it will commend to our hearts that great Redeemer who *hath borne our griefs, and carried our sorrows.* We shall look away from our desperate moral defilement, to that blood *which cleanseth from all sin;* from our weakness, to his strength; from our sins, to his perfect righteousness. It is but a little while, and he *that shall come will come, and will not tarry.* The day of our emancipation is fast approaching, when the *earthly house of this tabernacle* will be exchanged for *a building of God, a house not made with hands, eternal in the heavens.* The spirit shall no more be impeded by the disorders of the flesh, for this *vile body shall be fashioned like unto Christ's glorious body.*

But as godly Mason says, we are not to expect the sunshine of joy all through this vale of tears. Comfortable frames and joyful feelings, though sweet and delightful, are not always most profitable. Were we ever on the mount of joy, we should forget we are strangers and pilgrims on earth—be for building tabernacles of rest in a polluted place, and cry out with the highly favoured disciples, *it is good for us to be here.* But they knew not what they said. It is the glory of a Christian to live by faith on Jesus; to judge of his love by the word of truth, more than by sense and feeling;—yea, under dejection and disquiet of soul, to hope and trust in God; to check and rebuke one's self for doubts and diffidence, is the real exercise of faith. Thy frames may vary with the changes of thy health and of thy mortal part, but the foundation of God's love standeth sure. Thou mayest meet with many things from within and without to cast down and disquiet thee; but thou art called to look to Jesus, and say, Why art thou cast down, O my soul? and why art thou disquieted within me? Hope thou in God; for I shall yet praise him, who is the health of my countenance, and my God!

CHAPTER III.

TEMPTATIONS.

This is the very painting of your fears.—SHAKSPEARE.

Me oft hath fancy—
Myself creating what I saw.—COWPER.

THE apostle James reproves those who are too ready to connect their enticements to evil with supernatural causes; who ascribe to circumstances around them, an influence which proceeds from a susceptibility within them. *Let no man say when he is tempted, I am tempted of God, for God cannot be tempted of evil, neither tempteth he any man. But every man is tempted when he is drawn away by his own lusts and enticed.* The danger of walking among sparks belongs only to those who wear combustible garments. Nothing is more common among the desponding and morbid than a proneness to this very mistake. They impute their unhappy experiences to a cause which very often is only "the painting of their fears." How far the prince of tempters may take occasion, from their sickly physical state, to lead them into errors concerning their spiritual, we presume not to say. There is, however, the same intervention of second causes in their case, as in that which James speaks of. They are *drawn away* by their own bodily affections, and *enticed* into grave mistakes, which cause their many doubts and disquiet about their spiritual safety. It is a temptation of some, in their desponding state, to think that they have committed

THE SIN AGAINST THE HOLY GHOST.

We have known Christians, with eminent gifts, and piety which nobody doubted but themselves, who have been at times exceedingly distressed with the apprehension that they were guilty of this unpardonable sin. The perplexing question concerning its nature, than which, Father Austin said, "there was no harder in all the Scriptures," is clearly answered, as they suppose, in their own forlorn experience. Among the schoolmen of the middle ages there were no less than six different opinions about this fearful sin, all of which, in later times, have been rejected as erroneous. Calvin defined it a malicious resistance to divine truth, only for the sake of resistance. In this view Arminius concurred with Calvin, although opposed to him in so many others of more importance. Since the Reformation, a more common opinion has been, that it was the sin of the Jews when they ascribed the miracles of Christ to the agency of Satan. Dr. Chalmers and others, think it to be, not so much any one sin against the Holy Ghost, as a prolonged sinning—a resisting and grieving the heavenly Comforter until he ceases to strive, and withdraws; when the forsaken heart is left like a field on which the clouds shed no more rain. The good seed of the word will not take root and bring forth fruit in the former case, any more than *bare grain, wheat, or some other* will germinate, so long as the earth is *powder and dust* in the absence of proper moisture. Conviction of sin, regeneration, sanctification, are no longer possible, because the dishonoured Spirit, so often repelled, has let these impenitent persons alone. Sinning now has become unpardonable, as it can no longer be repented of, and not because it is, in its own nature, worse than it was before the Spirit's final exit. It does not come within the scope of the present volume to write a treatise on this grave subject; but it is introduced to the reader's notice only so far as to exhibit the moral effect of a physical cause. The gloomy prognosis in cases like these, is a token, not as the sufferers suppose, that they are unconverted, but that they are unwell. Mr. Kemper says, that in ninety-nine instances out of a hundred it is a symptom of bodily disease, "of which state Satan takes advantage to annoy and distress them. This appears," he adds, "for two reasons—first, that so many recover, become comfortable, and cease to charge themselves with the commission of that most frightful of all sins: the second is, that others know their characters to be better than they say they are, and from the unreasonable charges which they bring against themselves, which others, in their sober senses, can see were impossible." We once knew a young man, who had lived twelve years under the impression that he had survived his day of grace. He supposed that he could refer to the very day, and mention the act, by which he caused the Holy Spirit to withdraw, and leave him in a condition of hopeless obduracy. In all this time he had shown a becoming respect to the preaching of the gospel, but without any benefit of which he was conscious, or that was visible to others. No one suspected what was the state of his mind—not his pastor, nor most intimate friends; for in all his conversation he had carefully concealed it from both. But the Spirit that he had exiled for ever, as he imagined, was striving with him still, and at length constrained him to reveal this oppressive secret to his pastor. He was then told that the very distress of mind which had caused him to seek that interview, was at once the token and effect of the Holy Spirit's presence. The remark was supported by citation from the Scriptures, and followed by prayer. His mind was at once relieved, when his joy was now great in proportion to his former deep and long-continued sorrow. Dr. Ridgley says, that "such as are guilty of this sin have no conviction in their conscience of any crime committed herein; but stop their ears against all reproof, and often set themselves, with the greatest hatred and malice against those who, with faithfulness, admonish them to the contrary. That they go out of the way of God's ordinances, and willingly exclude themselves from the means of grace, which they treat with the utmost contempt, and use all means in their power that others may be deprived of them." A consciousness of sin then, according to Dr. Ridgley, a solicitude and sorrow produced by a person's fears of having sinned beyond pardon, are evidence that his case is not so desperate as he supposes. His "pain to find he cannot feel" is a symptom of vitality. It proves that he has not passed into the callous state of those whom the apostle Paul describes as *past feeling*. Some time before the Rev. Daniel Baker made a profession of religion, he was in great spiritual darkness, and on the borders of despair from the fear that he had sinned away his day of grace. "The unpardonable sin!—the unpardonable sin!—I was very much afraid that I had committed it; but one day, reading a book called 'Russel's Seven Sermons,' I met with a sentence in the last sermon which gave me great comfort. It was to this effect—that if a man has any serious concern about the salvation of his soul, and has a tender thought in relation to his Redeemer, that was proof positive that he had not committed the unpardonable sin. Immediately my burden was gone; every cloud was scattered, and my feelings became most delightful. It was like the beauty of spring after a long and dreary winter. I had new views of my Saviour; felt that I could rest upon him; and was enabled to *rejoice with joy unspeakable and full of glory.*" Another common temptation is to the

ADOPTION OF A FALSE STANDARD OF DUTY, OR OF AMBIGUOUS EVIDENCES OF A REGENERATE STATE.

Like the Jews who could not *discern the signs of the times* which were so visible in the moral firmament, and so intelligible to many, they asked for others that the Saviour would not give, and which they had no divine warrant to expect. Thus, how many have lost their spiritual peace by the sudden occurrence of an "alarming passage of Scripture," as if it were a supernatural warning. They forget that a bad spirit can suggest a text as well as the Good, and that its meaning is liable to be perverted in order that it may suit the morbid state of their mind when it is presented, just as water takes the colour of the soil over which it runs. It is mentioned in the life of Mr. Lackington, the celebrated bookseller, that when quite a youth, he was at one time locked up to prevent his attending a Methodist meeting in Taunton.

Under a strong mental impression that he ought to go, he opened his Bible for direction, when his eye caught the passage: *He shall give his angels charge concerning thee, and in their hand they shall bear thee up, lest thou dash thy foot against a stone.* This, Mr. Lackington says, "was quite enough for me; so, without a moment's hesitation, I ran up two pair of stairs to my own room, and out of the window I leaped, to the great terror of my poor mistress, who had charge of me." He was, of course, severely bruised, and confined to his bed fourteen days. Doubtless young Lackington was sincere, and was not aware of his adopting the very sense of the passage imposed on it by Satan, and which, in his excited state, he was so predisposed to receive. The great moral lesson which this experience taught him was never forgotten. Nor was it bought dearly, even at the expense of so much bodily peril. It is a striking exemplification of the folly of all who are, like him, enticed to bite the Tempter's hook when baited by a text of the Bible. Persons sometimes think themselves to be following a light from heaven, when they are led by a vain imagination and a deceiving heart. Others, again, trust to the evidence of "dreams," and are at one time alarmed, and at another comforted, by *thoughts from the visions of the night*, which they seem to believe are prompted by the same Spirit that addressed Eliphaz the Temanite: as if physiology had not made it too clear to be any longer doubted, that the character of our dreams depends very much upon our physical condition as affected by the amount or quality of our food last taken, and the state of our stomach. One man retiring to bed after a light meal, will dream of Paradise; while the digestive organs of another, gorged and oppressed by the excesses of the evening, will make him dream of perdition. Baron Trenck relates, that being almost dead with hunger when confined in his dungeon, his dreams every night presented to him the well filled and luxurious tables of Berlin, from which, as they were spread before him, he imagined he was about to relieve his hunger. Not a small proportion of our dreams at night are the prolonged waking thoughts of the day, and come, according to Solomon, *through the multitude of business.* Condorcet told some one, that while he was engaged in abstruse and profound calculations, he was frequently obliged to leave them in an unfinished state in order to retire to rest, and that the remaining steps, and the conclusion of his calculation, had more than once presented themselves in his dreams. Mr. Coleridge says, that after reading an account of the Khan Kubla, he fell into a sleep, and in that situation composed an entire poem of not less than two hundred lines, some of which he afterwards committed to writing. President Edwards so fully believed that our dreams are generally fashioned from the materials of the thoughts and feelings that we have while awake, that he used to take particular notice of his dreams, in order to ascertain from them what his predominant inclinations were. Such being the connection between the operations of our mind in sleep and our sensations and conceptions when awake, we see the error of those who are so ready to ascribe their dreams to a supernatural influence, and receive them as revealing the will of God. We once knew a lady, in advanced age, that gave little evidence of piety, who had cherished for many years an unwavering assurance of her salvation, which was based upon nothing but a dream. That God no longer informs men of his mind through supernatural dreams, as he did in patriarchal times, we do not assert. We presume to fix no limit to this method of divine communication—to say when it ceased; or that *old men do not dream dreams*, *and young men see visions* still. The apparent connection that is sometimes seen between men's dreams and the subsequent events which they seem to foresee and predict, is too striking and exact to be accidental or fortuitous, or to be explained "on simple and natural principles." A dream of this sort is mentioned in the memoir of a distinguished clergyman of England, to whom the facts were well known. A young lady, whose mind had become awakened to consider the subject of religion with special interest, dreamed of being in a place of worship, where she heard a sermon, but when she awoke, could remember nothing but the personal appearance of the preacher, and his text. The impression on her mind, however, was very deep, and she resolved on the next Lord's day morning to "find the place that she dreamed of, if she should go from one end of London to the other." About one o'clock she found herself in the heart of the city, where she dined, and afterwards set out again in search of this place of worship. About half-after-two o'clock she saw a great number of people going down the Old Jewry, and determining to see where they went, she was led by them to the meeting-house of the Rev. Mr. Shower. She had no sooner entered the door, than, turning to a companion, she said with some surprise, "This is the very place I saw in my dream." It was not long before Mr. Shower entered the pulpit, when, with greater surprise, she observed, "This is the very man I saw in my dream; and if every part of it holds true, he will take for his text the 7th verse of the

116th Psalm: *Return unto thy rest, O my soul, for the Lord hath dealt bountifully with thee.* When he arose to pray, every petition expressed the desire of her heart. Then followed the sermon, which, to her joyous amazement, was on the very passage which had been impressed on her mind in the dream. The result was her saving conversion, and her finding that *rest for her soul* which she had so long sought elsewhere in vain. Not less remarkable was the case mentioned by Dr. Abercrombie, of a most respectable clergyman in a country parish of Scotland, who made a collection in his church for an object of public benevolence, in which he felt deeply interested. The amount of the collection, which was received in ladles carried through the church, fell greatly short of his expectation; and during the evening of the day he frequently alluded to the fact with expressions of much disappointment. In the following night he dreamed that three one-pound notes had been left in one of the ladles, having been so compressed that they had stuck in the corner when the ladle was emptied. He was so impressed with the vision, that at an early hour in the morning he went to the church, found the ladle that he had seen in his dream, and drew from one of the corners of it, the three one-pound notes. The same writer gives an account of another clergyman, who had gone to Edinburgh from a short distance in the country, and was sleeping at an inn, when he dreamed of seeing a fire, and one of his children in the midst of it. He awoke with the impression, and instantly left town on his return home. When he arrived within sight of his house, he found it on fire, and got there in time to assist in saving one of his children, who, in the alarm and confusion, had been left in a state of danger. The authority on which we have the story forbids us to doubt its authenticity. But while there is now and then a case like these, which no philosophy of the mental powers can fully explain, yet the wild, grotesque, incoherent, and non-natural character of most, prove them

> To be the children of an idle brain,
> Begot of nothing but vain fantasy.

As the bard of Avon expounds the theory, under the whimsical fiction of Queen Mab sallying forth by night in her hazle-nut chariot, on her dream-inspiring missions—

When in this state, she gallops night by night
Through lovers' brains, and then they dream of love;
On courtiers' knees, that dream on court'sies straight;
O'er lawyers' fingers, who straight dream on fees;
O'er ladies' lips, who straight on kisses dream:
Sometimes she gallops o'er a courtier's nose,
And then dreams he of smelling out a suit;
And sometimes comes she with a tithe-pig's tail,
Tickling a parson's nose as 'a lies asleep,
Then dreams he of another benefice:
Sometimes she driveth o'er a soldier's neck,
And then he dreams of cutting foreign throats,
Of breaches, ambuscadoes, Spanish blades,
Of healths five fathom deep; and then anon
Drums in his ear; at which he starts, and wakes;
And, being thus frighted, swears a prayer or two,
And sleeps again.

Many Christians, of a nervous temperament, are tempted to make too much of

RELIGIOUS FRAMES.

They will imagine themselves, perhaps, to be in a state of favour with God, or to be unreconciled, according to their present impression or mental enjoyment. Mr. Brownlow North, in one of his public addresses in Ireland, mentioned the case of a female in Belfast, who said that she knew that Christ had pardoned her sins, because she was so happy; but if her feeling of happiness were taken away, she would not think her sins to have been forgiven. "Many imagine, unless they are at all times in a glow of fervour, an ecstatic frame of feeling, all must be wrong with them. But there is nothing more dangerous or deceptive than a life of mere feeling; and its *most* dangerous phase is a life of religious emotional excitement. It is in the last degree erroneous to consider all this glowing ecstacy of frame a necessary condition of healthful spiritual life. You will not be asked, in the last great day, whether you had great enjoyment, or much enlargement of soul here. Speak to that vast multitude which no man can number, now around the throne. Ask them whether they came through much *consolation* and joy in the Lord. No! through much tribulation. Ask them whether they were saved by their warmth of love to their Saviour. No! but they had washed their robes, and made them white in the blood of the Lamb." Many persons, Mr. North says, derive their faith from their feelings, whereas they ought to do the exact reverse, and let their feelings flow from their faith.

The power of temptation in the form we now speak of, was exemplified, to a remarkable extent, in the case of Mrs. Hawkes, that devoted friend of Mr. Cecil, of London, and an honoured servant of Christ. Her copious diary is full of meditations which exhibit her spiritual vacillancy, and show that this was her infirmity. Thus, after one of her transitions from spiritual gloom to light and hope, she exclaims: "How variable are our frames and feelings! How like the shining and the shadow passing over the green plain! But, blessed be God, our salvation consisteth not in frames and feelings, but in being engrafted on the living Vine, and abiding in Christ; consisteth not even in our sensible hold on him, but in our simple belief of his gracious declaration that he will *never leave, nor forsake*, nor suffer us to be plucked out of his hand." In reference to such cases as hers, Mr. Newton remarks, "that a humble, dependent frame of spirit, perseverance in the appointed means, care to avoid all occasions of sin, a sincere endeavour to glorify God, an eye to Jesus Christ as our *all in all*, are sure indications that the soul 'is thriving,' whether sensible consolation abound or not. Neither high nor low frames will do for a standard of faith; *self* may be strong in both." Persons who are conscious of such spiritual oscillations, should learn to discriminate between their emotions or frames and their habitual principles of action. The former may be likened to the little eddies near the margin of a river, which, at different times, flow towards all points of the compass. The latter are the current, constantly tending the same way, and which makes it evident in what direction the great volume of water is running. In one of his affectionate letters to Mrs. Hawkes that relates to the religious depression which she often suffered, he compares an afflicted believer to "a man that has an orchard laden with fruit, who, because the wind has blown off the leaves, sits down and weeps. If one asks, 'What do you weep for?' 'Why, my apple-leaves are gone!' 'But, have you not your apples left?' 'Yes.' 'Very well, then, do not grieve for a few leaves, which could only hinder the ripening of your fruit.' Pardon and promises, that cannot fail, lie at the root of your profession, my dear daughter; and fruits of faith, hope, and love, that no one can question, have long covered your branches. The east wind sometimes carries off a few leaves, though the *rough wind is stayed.* And what if every leaf were gone? What if not a single earthly comfort were left? Christ has prayed and promised that your fruit shall remain; and it shall be my joy to behold it in all eternity." Not less injurious to the spiritual progress of others, is a

HABIT OF MENTAL INTROSPECTION.

We mean, not the salutary practice of self-examination, which is commended alike by apostolic injunction and Christian experience. But we speak of a continual peering inward on their thoughts, emotions, affections, convictions of sin, and various exercises of mind, instead of looking away from them all to Christ. It is the natural proneness of a doubting and fearful mind, which it is often hard to resist. But, like Mary's visit to the sepulchre after the resurrection, it is a seeking of the living among the dead. Some persons, in their desponding moods, Mr. Spencer says, "think only of themselves and their sins. Nothing can magnify equal to melancholy—and nothing is so monotonous. A melancholy man, left to himself and the sway of his melancholy, will not have a new idea once a month. His thoughts will move round and round in the same dark circle. This will do him no good; he ought to get out of it. Depression never benefits body or soul. *We are saved by hope.*" But next in danger to this mistake of looking to themselves for help and light, is their "making a test of the experience of others for the trial of our own." In a letter to Mr. Anderson, Dr. Chalmers speaks of the besetting anxiety that attends such a practice, concerning which he makes the following excellent suggestions, as the promptings of his own observation and consciousness: "When you read books upon the subject of conversion, you see a certain process assigned, and in such a confident and authoritative way too, that you are apt to conceive that this is the very process, and that there can be no other. I compare it with my own history, and my own resolutions, and I am apt to be alarmed at the want of correspondence in a good many particulars. Scott's 'Force of Truth' is an example; Doddridge's 'Rise and Progress of Religion in the Soul' another; and last, though not least, the 'Pilgrim's Progress.' I pronounce them all to be excellent, and that there are many exemplifications such as they describe. But the process is not authoritative, nor is it universal. The Spirit taketh its own way with each individual, and you know it only by its fruits. I cannot say of myself that

I ever felt a state of mind corresponding to John Bunyan's Slough of Despond. Indeed, I blame myself most sincerely, that I cannot excite in my heart a high enough conception of sin in all its malignity. I hope I have the conviction, but I cannot command the degree of emotion that I should like; and in the hardness of a heart, not so tenderly alive, as it ought to be, to the authority of my Lawgiver, and the enormity of trampling upon him, I feel how far, and very far I am at this moment from *the measure of the stature of the perfect man in Christ Jesus our Lord.* Now, what am I to infer from this?—that I have not yet surmounted the impassable barrier which stands between me and the gate of life? So one would suppose from John Bunyan, and so I would suppose myself, were it not for the kind assurance of my Saviour, whose every testimony is truth, and every tone is tenderness: *He that believeth in me, though he were dead, yet shall he live.* This is my firm hold, and I will not let it go. I sicken at all my own imperfect preparations. I take one deci sive and immediate step, and resign my all to the sufficiency of my Saviour." Many Christians, of unequal experience, are wont to

Make an idol of comfort.

This temptation is akin to that already mentioned, which rests the believer's hope on the unstable basis of frames. But it implies an erroneous view of the Scriptures, and a mistake of the only source from which solid and enduring comfort can ever emanate. In his life, written by Clarke, Dr. Harris is quoted as exposing, with much discrimination, this among other mistakes of disturbed minds that are seeking relief. "What an idol," he says, "do some make of comfort, as if it were their Christ?" It absorbs their thoughts, and they seem to care for nothing but this. And when their comfort comes, they are apt to lose it—some by nourishing too great scrupulosity, and others by contracting carelessness and hardness of heart. But if we miss or lose our comforts for other causes than our own remarkable default and disobedience, we must acquiesce in the pleasure of God till the blessed day dawns.

But why look so intently after this, when, if we study and understand the covenant of grace, and are but sincere, it will give us quietness under our manifold infirmities and trials, even though comforts flow not in upon us? But another error of these seekers after comfort is to mistake its abatement for an absolute removal. In some cases, perhaps, their fears may be just; and yet many are ready to mistrust the least declension of it for its loss. They ought to understand that comfort long enjoyed does not make the impression it did at first—especially if they came out of great darkness; for then it is like standing in the open sun, after having just come out of a dungeon. The change, at first, is very impressive; but after a long and habitual sunshine, though the heat and benign influences are just the same, yet use and time abate gradually the transports of the sensation." Hence the peace of such believers, unlike the steady flow of a river, is as unstable as the waters of the always changing ocean. Many excellent Christians, in reading the teachings of Christ, appear to make the same mistake as did the sons of Zebedee; they are looking for their crown without the antecedent cross—for the victory of faith, without the *good fight* through which Paul gained it, and everybody else, who has gained it at all. In their desire to be *filled with comfort*, which is one of the fruits of sanctification, they lose sight of the process of trial by which God is pleased, in most cases, to carry on and mature this work of the Spirit. Such mistaken disciples expect to enjoy, in the present life, Mason says, that unmingled happiness which God has promised only for the future. 'O, give me comforts, or I die!' saith the soul of such an one; 'for surely, were I a child of God, I should not be thus tried, afflicted, and distressed.' 'Nay,' saith the Saviour, 'ye know not what ye ask. Dost thou forget *the exhortation which speaketh unto you as unto children, despise not thou the chastening of the Lord, nor faint when thou art rebuked of him.* Did I bid thee believe on me? Believe also my words; *through much tribulation* thou must enter my kingdom.' We often pray, like Peter, to be excused being washed by our Lord; but we consider neither his love nor our own advantage. *If I wash thee not, thou hast no part with me. If ye be without chastisement, then are ye not sons. I will purge away thy dross and thy tin, and purify thee in the furnace.* Then shall thy graces shine brighter, thy faith grow stronger, thy love burn more fervent, and thy obedience be more cheerful. O happy to live, not so much on comforts, as on the God of all comforts." But the worst of all forms of temptation, is when it tends to

DESPAIR.

The unhappy condition of which we have treated, assumes many phases, and is modified by circumstances almost numberless. In all cases it is attended with mental suffering more or less aggravated; but the malady sometimes reaches its dreadful climax in a state of despair. In most instances of this kind, the symptoms of bodily disease are so apparent, that all religious counsels may be deferred as superfluous, until the physical state has been changed by proper medical treatment. Sometimes, however, when there are no perceptible indications of impaired health, the mind sinks into a state of hopelessness, which is promoted and nurtured by perverted views of truth, or a misapplication of its meaning. They are afraid to pray, perhaps, because *the sacrifice of the wicked is abomination;* or at some former time they may have *eaten and drunk damnation to themselves* by partaking *unworthily* at the Lord's table. Not long ago a pastor told me of an interesting female member of his church, who had been despairing of her salvation many years, because of her having been guilty, as she supposed, of this presumptuous act. Very often, in this sickly state, the mind is tempted to ponder the divine decrees, or the mystery of election, or try to reconcile the divine purposes and foreknowledge with human free agency. It endeavours to "pry between the folded leaves" of the book of life, which is forbidden even to Gabriel; to comprehend that which is incomprehensible, and to know that which *passeth knowledge.* The forlornness and desperation that such diseased musings lead to, are indescribable. But cases of this kind so closely resemble those in which the mind is brooding over an imagined sin against the Holy Ghost, that the counsels addressed to the former are not less adapted to instruct the latter. Persons under the power of temptation in this form, not only neglect the means of grace, but, by a constant rumination on their wretchedness, only make it the more difficult to dislodge the delusion, and minister effectual relief. But "despair never made a human being better; it has made many a devil worse." Mr. Spencer says, that at one time there was in his congregation a woman about forty years of age, who was a wonder to me. She was one of the most intelligent and well educated of the people; she had been brought up from her childhood in the family of a clergyman, as his daughter; was very attentive to the observance of the Sabbath; and was never absent from her seat in the church. As the mother of a family she had few equals. Everybody respected her. But she was not a member of the church; and whenever I had endeavoured to call attention to the subject, she was so reserved, that I could not even conjecture what was her particular state of mind. I was told that she never spoke to any one in respect to her religious feelings. One day I called upon her, and frankly told her my embarrassment about her. I mentioned her uniform taciturnity; my motive in aiming to overcome it; my supposition that some error kept her from religion, and my inability to conjecture what it was. I said to her that I had not a doubt there was something locked up in her own mind which she never whispered to me. She seemed very much surprised at this declaration, and I instantly asked her if it was not so? With some reluctance she confessed it was. And then, after no little urgency, she said she would tell me the whole—not on her own account—but that her case might not discourage me from aiming to lead others to Christ. She then said that her day of grace was past; that she had had every possible opportunity for salvation; that every possible motive had been a thousand times presented to her; that she had been the subject of deep convictions and anxiety often; she had lived through three remarkable revivals of religion, in which many of her companions had been led to Christ; and that she had again and again attempted to work out her salvation, but all in vain. "I know my day is gone," she said, "and I am given over." She spoke this in a decided manner, solemnly and coldly, unmoved as a rock. As I was silently thinking for a moment how I could best remove her error, she went on to say that she had never before now mentioned this; that she fully believed in the reality of experimental religion, and assented to everything she had ever heard me preach, except when once or twice I had spoken of religious despair. But inasmuch as her day of grace was past, she did not wish to have her mind troubled on the subject of religion at all, and asked me to say nothing more about it. I inquired how long she had been in this state of mind? She told me she had known for eighteen years that there was no salvation for her. I inquired if she ever prayed? She said she had not prayed for eighteen years. I asked if she did not feel unhappy to be in such a state? She said she seldom thought of it, as it would do no good; and she never intended to think of it again. I called to see her time after time about once a week for six weeks; examined all her reasons for thinking that her day of grace had gone by, except one, and convinced her that they were false. Evidently she had become intellectually interested; there was but one point left. She had never, at any preceding interview, expressed a wish to see me, or asked me to call again. I now called her attention summarily to the ground we had gone over, and how she had found all her *refuges of lies* swept away, save one, as she herself had acknowledged; and if that were gone, she would think her salvation possible. I then asked her if she wished to see me again? She replied that her opinion was unchanged, but that she would like to hear what I had to say about the remaining point, which, as she truly said, I had avoided so often. I called the next day, and took up the one point left—this last item which doomed her to despair. As I examined it, reasoning with her, and asking if she thought me right from step to step as I went on, the intensity of her thoughts became painful to me. She gazed upon me with unutterable astonishment. Her former cold and stone-like appearance was gone; her bosom heaved with emotion; and her whole frame seemed agitated with a new kind of life. To see the dreadful fixedness of despair melting away from her countenance, and the dawnings of inceptive hope taking its place, was a new and strange thing to me. It looked like putting life into a corpse. As my explanation and argument drew towards the close, she turned pale as death. She almost ceased to breathe; and when I had finished, and in answer to my question, she confessed that she had no reason to believe that her day of grace was past, and instantly she looked as if she had waked up in a new world. The tears gushed from her eyes in a torrent, she clasped her hands, sprung from her seat, and walked back and forth across the room, exclaiming, "I can be saved!—I can be saved!—I can be saved!" She was so entirely overcome that I thought she would faint, or perhaps her reason give way. I was afraid to leave her, and remained, saying nothing, till she became more composed, when, with a silent bow, I withdrew. The next Sabbath morning she was at the meeting for inquirers, and appeared like other awakened sinners, with nothing remarkable about her except her manifest determination to seek the Lord with all her heart. In about three weeks she became one of the happiest creatures in hope, I ever saw. She afterwards united with the church, and yet lives a happy and decided believer.

CHAPTER IV.

COUNSELS.

'Tis hard, in such a strife of rules, to choose
The best.
ARMSTRONG.

HAVING examined the nature of physical causes, their influence upon religious experience, and the uses of knowledge, we come now to the most important department of our subject, viz.

THE COUNSELS WHICH SUCH CASES OF SUFFERING REQUIRE.

And here we should repeat the remark, that as we are not writing for medical men, neither do we affect the medical knowledge which is required to do it justice in all its bearings. The most which has been proposed and attempted, is to offer the results of some experience and observation in prosecuting the ministry, rather than the fruits of scientific research. Without much of the latter, it has appeared to the writer, that there is ample scope for some profitable suggestions, by which the unhappy condition of many may be reached and relieved.

The more conversant we become with the varied cases of spiritual disquietude, occurrent in our churches, the more occasion we see for all the aid which may be furnished by the counsels and experience of others. That this should have been made no more frequently the subject of discussion by the pen or the pulpit, is to be ascribed, not to its intrinsic barrenness, nor its want of importance, as is evident from the prominency given it in the older English writers, but the demand for treatises on subjects like that of our present discussion is small, and for the most part restricted to those whose cases are portrayed, and very often to a smaller number even than they. Sometimes there is such an utter prostration of all energy, intellectual and moral, in the afflicted themselves, that it is extremely difficult to arrest their attention even by instructions, which, if heeded, would relieve their spirits, and restore them to cheerfulness.

"In perusing the memoirs of those who have devoted themselves to God," Dr. Cheyne says, "nothing has appeared to us more remarkable than their ignorance of, or inattention to, many of those things which affect their spiritual enjoyment; and especially that physical causes should be so continually overlooked by those who must be fully aware of the influence which the body exercises over the mind, and the mind over the body, in all men, but particularly in Christians." They are habitually desponding and unhappy; not appearing to know how much the pleasurable emotions of the soul are dependent on the state of the health.

Non est vivere, sed valere, vita.
Existence is not life, but to be well.

To those, then, who are perplexed about their spiritual state, and are often fearful and sad, we would say,

Endeavour, so far as possible, to ascertain the true cause of your doubts and spiritual troubles.

This is Baxter's prescription. "If you should mistake in the cause," he says, "it would much frustrate the most excellent means for cure. The very same doubts and complaints may come from several causes in several persons, and therefore admit not of the same way of cure. Sometimes the cause begins in the body, and thence proceedeth to the mind; sometimes it begins in the mind, and thence distempereth the body. Again, it proceedeth from wordly crosses, or scruples upon points of religious doctrine, decays of inward grace, or, as it was with David, from the deep wounds of some scandalous sin. Which of these is your own case, you must be careful to find out, and apply the means for cure accordingly. And if, upon close and careful examination, it prove like Achan's fraud, to be some latent sin, then relief can only come (as it infallibly will come,) by putting it away. If the cause be found in the state of your health, then acquit your soul from all that part of your disquietness which proceeds from this source; remembering in all your self-examinations, self-judgings, and reflections on your heart, that it is not directly to be charged with those sorrows that come from your spleen, save only remotely, as all other diseases are the fruits of sin, as a lethargic dullness is the deserved fruit of sin; but he that should charge it immediately on his soul, would wrong himself, and he that would attempt the cure, must do it on the body."

It is admitted that such counsel as this is attended with more or less danger; that it may encourage presumption in some, and thus lead them to heal the hurt of their spirit too slightly and hastily, by resolving it into a cause over which they have no control, and for which they are not accountable. How many pains which afflict the soul, especially in later life, are only retributory. They are the *bitter things* in which the sufferer is *made to possess the iniquities of his youth;* "the physical results of early crime in the disease and infirmity of the body; the mental results, in the weakness, disorder, and unsettledness of the intellect; and the moral results, in the hardness, impenitency, and unbelief of the soul." And although the petulance, impatience, repining, and restive spirit which they often produce, are the effect of a physical cause, yet they are not blameless, and are no more to be ascribed to the mere sovereignty or providence of God, than is the delirium tremens of the drunkard, or the death of the suicide. It is hoped that the subject has been sufficiently guarded against this perversion, by what has been said in the preceding chapter. Unhappily, however, as has also been intimated before, many of those who need such instructions, are too dejected and inert to be aroused to make any serious and persevering inquiry after the source of their despondency. "To reason with a man against the views which arise from melancholy," Dr. Alexander says, "is commonly as inefficacious as reasoning against bodily pain. I have long made this a criterion, to ascertain whether the dejection experienced was owing to a physical cause; for in that case, argument, though demonstrative, had no effect." Very many are predisposed to take it for granted that their gloom proceeds from a culpable cause, whatever it may be;

that the more they should investigate the painful subject, the more they would discover to convince them that they were deceiving themselves, and that they had never been spiritually changed. But let no professor of religion in his senses ever be tempted to dispose of his own case in this precipitate and summary way. To give indulgence to such a lethargic ease, while in doubt about his salvation, is evidence of a sort of hallucination, which, instead of impairing his responsibility, greatly increases both his danger and his guilt. Let the inquiry into his own personal state, then, be pursued diligently, until he come to a satisfactory conclusion; let him persevere under a persuasion of the ineffable importance of the duty, as involving all that is desirable or fearful in the disclosures of eternity. His despondency may be produced by false views of religion, or these erroneous views may generate despondency. Nor is it in every case easy to determine which is cause and which is effect; the manner in which mind and body reciprocally act upon each other being often so inscrutable as to baffle the attempt to distinguish between physical and mental causes. "Where despondency puts on a religious form, its real nature may be ascertained by inquiring into the actual character and circumstances of the sufferer. Where there is palpable illusion, there is disease. False impressions may proceed from ignorance and misapprehension, and such impressions will yield to moral treatment. But if the notions are not merely inaccurate, but illusive; if the mind is found to have shaped out for itself the ideal object of its desponding apprehension, there can be no ground for hesitation in pronouncing the depression to be bodily distemper. There are morbid states of mind which do not rise to that height of nervous disorder which produces hallucination, but which still indicate an unhealthy state of body. There is such a thing as the religious vapours, for which the Pharmacopœia prescribes suitable remedies. But no one who knows what melancholy is, will confound that terrible visitation with any self-

16*

inflicted or fantastic complaints." Our second counsel to those who are thus afflicted, is to

AVAIL THEMSELVES OF JUDICIOUS MEDICAL ADVICE.

We refer in this direction more particularly to those whose state of doubting and darkness has been long continued. As in the case of Dr. Rush, the cause may exist in a morbid condition of the body, without being even suspected by themselves. To those whose trouble proceeds from this source, Baxter says again, "expect not that rational or spiritual remedies should suffice for your cure, any more than that a good sermon or comfortable words should cure the falling sickness, or palsy, or a broken head; for your melancholy fears are as really a bodily disease as the other, only because these work on the spirits and fantasy, on which words of advice do also work to a certain extent; therefore such words, and Scripture and reason may somewhat resist it, and may palliate and allay some of the effects at the present, but as soon as time hath worn off the force and effects of these reasons, the distemper presently returns."

As the cause therefore is in the animal part, it must be reached, if at all, by remedies which it comes more within the province of the medical than the spiritual counsellor to prescribe. The physician, it is true, cannot cure the moral cause that preys upon the mind, and, through that medium, injures the body, but he can, in a great measure, prevent the reaction of the body on the mind, by which reaction the moral affliction is rendered infinitely more difficult to bear. But let it not be forgotten that not every physician, how skilful soever, and learned, and successful in his general practice, is qualified to instruct the description of patients whom these remarks contemplate. No person has such opportunities of studying the mutual and reciprocating relationship between the mind and body, and yet it is one on which many of the faculty betray the most culpable ignorance. They want the "ability of searching out and understanding the moral causes of disease; they cannot read the book of the heart; and yet it is in this book that are inscribed, day by day, and hour by hour, all the griefs, and all the miseries, and all the vanities, and all the fears, and all the joys, and all the hopes of man, and in which will be found the most active and incessant principle of that frightful series of organic changes which constitute pathology. Many a disease is the *contre coup* (counter blow,) so to speak, of a strong moral emotion. The mischief may not be apparent at the time, but its germ will be, nevertheless, inevitably laid." Such sentiments from an eminent lecturer in one of the best medical schools of Europe, show the importance of special care and discretion in the choice of a physician for a malady which, by their own confession, so few understand, or know how to treat. Mr. Rogers advises all the afflicted of this sort to apply to doctors not only learned in the profession of physic, but who have themselves felt the disease; for it is impossible fully to understand the nature of it any other way than by experience: and that person, he says, is highly to be valued, whose endeavours God will bless to the removal of a complaint so obstinate and violent. How much evil has resulted from the injudicious counsel of incompetent advisers who can compute?

Infeliciter ægrotat, ubi plus est periculi, a medicamento quam a morbo.

It is a sad condition for the sick, when they are put in greater peril by their treatment, than by their disease.

Such, however, has been the change of late years in the character of diseases, and especially so great has been the increase of those by which the mind and spiritual affections are disturbed, that cases of this sort are better understood, and the number of competent advisers among the faculty is much greater than it was formerly. It is an interesting fact, which is not generally known, that a large proportion of our more serious ailments fall within the category to which we now refer.

Near the close of the seventeenth century, Sydenham estimated fevers to constitute, at that time, two-thirds of the diseases of mankind. About seventy years afterwards, Dr. Cheyne made nervous disorders about one-third of the complaints of the higher class in England. At the beginning of the nineteenth century, Trotter supposed them to constitute full two-thirds of all those which afflicted civilized society. And a later writer still, expresses the opinion that even Trotter's estimate falls below the truth. Of the four hundred thousand persons who died in England during 1856, one out of every eight died of diseases of the brain and nerves; and one out of every sixteen died of diseases of the digestive organs. We do not pretend to decide as to the comparative accuracy of these computations. It is enough to say, that the lowest is sufficiently great to appal, and also to show, that no department of the healing art claims more earnestly the attention of physicians than this. If the connection between the mind and body be so intimate as has been shown, the reasonableness of this resort for medical advice would be obvious, even if its practical value had not been tested by common experience. How often have we known a morbid condition of the mind or spirits to be as speedily and as effectually removed by the operation of a drug as a pain in the head. That peevishness, impatience, and irritability which make one intolerable to himself as well as to others, we see daily relieved by the same simple agency, as by the power of magic; and hence "our domestic happiness often depends on the state of the biliary and digestive organs; and the little disturbances of conjugal life may sometimes be more efficaciously cured by the physician than by the moralist; for a sermon or homily misapplied will never act so directly as a sharp medicine."

A physician in the city of Philadelphia was recently invited to visit a lady enjoying apparent health, living in affluence, and surrounded with everything which wealth and elevated condition, and affectionate friends could confer to render her happy; yet in the midst of it all she felt indescribably wretched, and sent for her medical adviser to explain the cause. It was a case of plethoric tendency, which called for depletion. A moderate bleeding afforded relief, and in a very few days she was restored to her former cheerfulness.

The Rev. M. B. Hope, M.D., in a well written Essay on Religious Melancholy, mentions the case of a young lady, who had been long and intimately known to the writer, who was "of a temperament highly nervous and sanguine, and embarked very young, with all her ardour, in the gay pleasures of fashionable life. A single season convinced her fully of their emptiness and folly. She was soon after brought under the influence of pungent preaching, and convinced of sin. The struggle was sharp and long; but the result was, that she gave herself, with all her heart, to a course of rigid religious duties. Above all, she seemed to live in an atmosphere of prayer. Her faith in the truth and promises of God, was without the shadow of a cloud. And yet she had not the pure enjoyment which she supposed to be the necessary fruit of real piety. She did not, therefore, look upon herself as a child of God; and her consequent anxiety wore upon her spirit, and secretly undermined her health. At length, one day, as she rose from prayer, the thought struck her like a thunderbolt, 'what if there is no God after all.' She repelled the thought with horror, and went her way. But the shock had struck from her hand 'the shield of faith,' and all her efforts were unable to grasp it again. From henceforth she found herself exposed to a constant shower of darts, fiery and poisoned, and she could not resist them. They stuck fast in her vitals, and drank up her spirits. The poison thus injected into the heart of her religious experience soon spread, and blighted the whole. She never knew a moment's peace, when her thoughts were upon her once favourite, and still engrossing subject. She called herself an infidel, and applied to herself the dreadful threatenings and doom of the unbeliever. And yet it was evident she was not, in any sense, an unbeliever. She was one of the most devout and consistent persons we ever knew. She was conscientious even to scrupulosity. She was a most devoted and faithful Sunday-school teacher, and God blessed her labours to the conversion of nearly all her scholars. She rejoiced to hear of persons becoming Christians, and would often say, with despair in her tones, how she envied them. When any of her acquaintances died without giving good evidence of piety she became excited, and as she expressed it, was ready to scream aloud. She gave every possible evidence that she had not, in reality, a shadow of a doubt about the truth of revelation. And yet no one ever dreamed that her difficulties were connected with disease of any sort; for her mind was remarkably clear, and active. The advice of pious friends and ministers, therefore, based upon the supposition that her case was one of spiritual darkness, or satanic temptation, was to persevere in prayer—to struggle on more earnestly, and God would give her light after he had tried her faith and patience and love. But the more she prayed and struggled the worse she grew. She would come from her closet, exhausted with the fearful conflict, and looking ready to sink into utter despair. The Sabbath was always the worst day of the week; and the labour and exhaustion of teaching aggravated her symptoms.

The only treatment which was successful,

in this case, would by many have been rejected with horror. She was advised to give up the struggle which she had maintained so unequally, and which would only have resulted in disastrous consequences—to think as little as possible on the subject—to spend less time in devotional exercises, and allow her mind to gather its scattered strength by relaxation. The form of prayer advised was short and audible, and such as took for granted what she had been struggling to convince herself of. Incessant pains were taken to present the character of God in a simple, affectionate, parental light, when anything led to the subject. The simplicity of faith, and the certainty of salvation, were occasionally flashed across her mind, when it was in a suitable frame. The only two evidences of piety which her state of mind rendered available, were kept prominent as the basis of new feelings and hopes, viz. her love to the people of God, and the pain she felt in the absence of divine favour, and the longing for its return. These were untouched by the dismal monster that had preyed upon her hopes.

By a judicious perseverance in a course like this, accompanied with well directed hygienic measures, suitable recreation, exercise, and diet, for improving her general health, and especially the tone of her nervous system, the mental energies began to react, and new views of truth and new hopes spring up in her mind."

Another case, furnished by the same, and adduced for the sake of showing the efficacy of judicious medical treatment, is that of "a lady, whose state of mind had baffled every attempt made by her judicious husband, to bring her relief. She was a woman of great refinement and strength of mind, eminently pious, and devoted to her interesting young family, whose education she conducted herself. While conferring every accomplishment upon her children, she was mainly anxious for their spiritual welfare. When we saw her, she was intensely excited, and had slept little for several nights. She said she had lost all interest in the instruction of her children, and had become utterly regardless of their personal appearance and her own. Her whole thoughts and feelings were engrossed about their salvation, her anxiety for which had become insupportably agonizing. When instructing, or dressing, or leading them out for their accustomed exercise, she was incessantly distracted with the thought, what good will all this do, while they are still impenitent! Though her flushed face and flashing restless eye, indicated strong physical excitement, yet her mind was so clear on every subject, and all her views so rational, that we attributed the whole difficulty to excessive and protracted anxiety, for an object of peculiar interest to a pious mother— the salvation of her children. We made repeated attempts to reason with her on the error and evils of her present state of mind. She admitted fully the justice of our reasoning, and concurred in the truth of all our positions, but we found that this was of no avail. Her excitement continued, and with it her distress, and all her difficulties. It appeared like a case of pure religious excitement, and was so looked upon by all her family. They did not deem her deranged, but it was evident she soon would be, unless relieved. Finding reasoning of no avail, and the excitement still increasing, we became convinced, on minute examination, that the whole difficulty originated, not in religious views or feelings at all, but in a morbid increase of arterial action, arising from some physical cause. One-twelfth of a grain of tartar emetic, five or six times a day, gave perfect relief, and restored both her views and feelings to the healthy standard."

Dryden, whose mind, notwithstanding its capacity for elevated and brilliant conceptions, was sometimes turbid and dull, well knew the utility of medical expedients as auxiliary to thought. "When I have a grand design before me," says he, "I ever take physic and let blood; for when you would have pure swiftness of thought and fiery flights of fancy, you must have a care of the pensive part, and for this, get help from the apothecary." Descartes, the philosopher, went farther still, and asserted that if any means can be found to render men wiser and more ingenious than they have been hitherto, such a method must be sought from the assistance of medicine: and Plutarch, speaking of the reaction of the mind upon the body as the cause of those injuries which it requires medicine to repair, very playfully observes, that "should the body sue the mind before a court of judicature for damages, it would be found that the mind had proved to be a ruinous tenant to its landlord."

None, we trust, will infer from what has thus been said of medical assistance, that we approve of that habitual tampering with drugs, or the injudicious perusal of medical books, which is so common with the nervous valetudinarian, by which he only makes his malady the worse.

> Exuperat magis, ægrescitque medendo.
> The disease is aggravated by the means used to cure it.

Rousseau admitted that this was a powerful cause of hypochondria in respect to himself. "Having read," he says, "a little on physiology, I set about studying anatomy; and passing in review the number and varied actions of the parts which compose my frame, I expected twenty times a day to feel them going wrong. Far from being astonished at finding myself dying, my wonder was that I could live at all. I did not read the description of any disease which I did not imagine myself to be affected with; and I am sure that if I had not been ill, I must have become so from this fatal study. Finding in every complaint the symptoms of my own, I believed I had got them all, and thereby added another still more intolerable, the fantasy of curing myself." All this private empiricism we would discourage, by directing the sufferer away from these experiments upon himself, to the well-taught physician, that more competent counsellor, who has been designated by Providence. Another important auxiliary to the desponding Christian is

SUITABLE SOCIETY,

or habitual intercourse with others, and especially the devout, who possess a happier temperament.

——— Whatever cheerful and serene
Supports the mind, supports the body too.

The influence of sympathy, its operation for both evil and good, is familiarly known. "We are all," says Locke, "a kind of chameleon, who take a moral tinge from the objects which surround us." The manifestation of fear or of confidence and self-possession in a time of danger, inspires a corresponding emotion in those who behold it. The "quid times? Cæsarem vehis," or Cæsar's appeal to the affrighted shipmaster, not to be afraid while he was aboard, will occur as a striking illustration; and how we all assimilate in character, as well as in manners, to those with whom we associate, is a fact of daily observation. Hence the salutary effect of a cheerful, sanguine Christian, upon those who are prone to melancholy. *As iron sharpeneth iron, so a man sharpeneth the countenance of his friend.* His society is exhilarating, like the wine prescribed by Solomon *to those that be of heavy* hearts. An interview with those of their own morbid tendencies may be advantageous sometimes, by correcting the usual mistake of such believers, that their case is peculiar, or has certain unfavourable characteristics, by which it is placed without the reach of the ordinary means of relief. A comparison of exercises and sentiments is often productive of good, in showing that their condition is not so singular as they had imagined. It is very hard indeed to persuade a person under great pain and anguish, and the sense of the wrath of God, and a fear of hell, that ever any has heretofore been so perplexed as he. Such, generally, think themselves worse than Cain, or Judas, or Simon Magus, and that their sins have greater aggravation. Mr. Rogers says, "I have known several that were long afflicted with trouble of mind, and melancholy—as Mr. Rosewell and Mr. Porter—both ministers, the latter whereof was six years oppressed with this distemper; yet afterwards both rejoiced in the light of God's countenance. I myself was near two years in great pain of body, and greater pain of soul, and without any prospect of peace or help; and yet God hath revived me in his sovereign grace and mercy; and there have been several heretofore sorely perplexed with great inward and outward trouble, whom God after that wonderfully refreshed. Mr. Robert Bruce, some time ago minister at Edinburgh, was twenty years in terrors of conscience, and yet delivered afterwards." From the prevailing lack of sympathy with which such sufferers meet, many prefer to hide their sorrows in their own bosom, to the risk of opening their heart to those who could poorly appreciate an experience so foreign to their own. Thus the late Captain Benjamin Wickes, of Philadelphia, concealed his long and oppressive melancholy for nearly twenty years, until it was discovered by that devoted servant of Christ, Mr. Joseph Eastburn, whose affectionate conversation and judicious counsels were the means of affording immediate relief.

How far the distressing symptoms of Cowper's malady were mitigated by the delightful society of the Unwins, is easily inferred from his memoirs; nor are any of us so imperturbable in our spiritual temperament, as not to be more or less lifted up or depressed by the joy or sadness of those Christian friends with whom we mingle. And hence one of four cardinal rules which the eminent casuist already quoted, has given to melancholy Christians, is to "keep company with the more cheerful sort of the godly; converse with men of the strongest faith, that have much of the heavenly mirth of believers, which faith doth fetch from the blood of Christ and from the promises of his word, and who can speak experimentally of the joy of the Holy Ghost, and these will be a great help to the reviving of your spirit and changing your melancholy habit, so far as without a physician it may be expected." On the other hand, decline, so far as practicable, the society of the gloomy and disconsolate. Their sorrowful spirit, like an evil distemper, is contagious, and your influence upon each other will be reciprocally prejudicial.

Oderunt hilarem tristes, tristemque jocosi.

The grave dislike the cheerful, and the merry hate the grave.

Some physiologists contend that laughter, as one of the greatest aids to digestion, is highly conducive to health, and therefore Hufeland, physician to the king of Prussia, commends the wisdom of the ancients, who maintained a jester, that was always present at their meals, "whose quips and cranks would keep the table in a roar." Dr. Everard Maynwaring, in his "Tutela Sanitatis," published in 1663, tells his melancholy patients to walk in the green fields, orchards, parks, and gardens—to avoid solitariness, and keep merry company. In the chapter entitled "Hygiastic Precautions and Rules appropriate to the various Passions of Mind," he says: "Mirth subtiliates, purifies, and cheers the spirits; puts them upon activity that before were torpid, dull, and heavy, and excites them to operation and duty in the several faculties; volatizeth, rarifies, and attenuates gross, feculent, obstructing humours; preserves youth, vigour, and beauty; makes the body plump and fat, by expanding the spirits into the external parts, and conveying nutriment, whose wholesome effects are much the same with those of exercise, and may well supply when that is wanting.

Dum fata sinunt vivite læti.—SENECA.

While the fates permit, let your life be cheerful."

Such counsel, quoted from the old Roman philosopher, on whom Father Jerome bestows such extravagant praise, is much better than some of his instructions for carrying it into effect. But how much wiser the teaching of Paul, who would provide against a large proportion of our disquietudes in life, by a removal of the cause. We are prone to look no further than to our own case, as if it were peculiar, and nobody ever suffered in the same way, or to the same extent, with ourselves. But this, the apostle teaches, is as impolitic as it is selfish. *Look not every man on his own things, but every man also on the things of others.* Do not dwell in perpetual meditation on the ills that afflict yourselves, but turn your thoughts sometimes to the incomparably greater trials of others. Your mind may be depressed and sad under the influence of some imagined or real malady, but is it not because you forget how much better is your condition than that of many whose "days are blackness, whose every breath is in suffering, and who feed on tears?" You may not possess your wonted ease of locomotion, and perhaps spend many long days and nights in great pain. But what is all that you endure, a hundred-fold increased, compared with the bitter cup of such a poor suffering cripple as is mentioned by Dr. Hall, who, he says, is still living (1859) at the age of forty-five, with every joint in his body as immovable as a solid bone, except those of two toes and two fingers. His jaws have been set and motionless for thirty years, the only aperture through which he receives food being that made by the falling out of his front teeth. In the *Journal of Health* for 1859, is a sprightly letter to the editor from a correspondent in Virginia, who describes himself as rigid and helpless as a mass of stone; his eyes and tongue being the only members over which he has the least control. "My digestive organs," he writes, "have lost their activity, and I have a distressing asthmatic affection. The inability to open my jaws forces me to subsist upon such food as I can compress through a cavity made by the loss of two of my teeth." But the aspect of his letter is bright and genial, indicating a livelier sense of the Divine beneficence than thousands show, who have health and everything around them to make life happy. Examples of such utter physical disability in the organs of the body, and derangement of their functions, are comparatively rare. But what a rebuke do they minister to the thousands of murmurers who habitually undervalue the blessings of Providence, because their abundance and commonness make them so familiar. One of the happiest persons we ever heard of, was a lady who was so prostrated by palsy that she had no power over a limb or muscle from her neck downwards, and could move no part of her whole person but her head. Dr. Paley says, that one great cause of our insensibility to the goodness of the Creator, is the very *extensiveness* of his bounty. We prize but little what we share only in common with the rest, or with the generality of our species. When we hear of blessings, we think forthwith of successes, of prosperous fortunes, of honours, riches, preferments—*i. e.* of those advantages and superiorities over others which we happen either to possess or to be in pursuit of, or to covet. The *common* benefits of our nature entirely escape us. Yet these are the great things. These constitute what most properly ought to be accounted blessings of Providence; what alone, if we might so speak, are worthy of its care. Nightly rest and daily bread, the ordinary use of our limbs, and senses, and understandings, are gifts which admit of no comparison with any other. Yet, because almost every man we meet with possesses these, we leave them out of our enumeration; they raise no sentiment, they move no gratitude. Now, herein is our judgment perverted by our selfishness. A blessing ought, in truth, to be the *more* satisfactory—the bounty at least of the donor is rendered more conspicuous by its very diffusion, its commonness, its cheapness; by its falling to the lot, and forming the happiness of the great bulk and body of our species, as well as ourselves. Nay, even when we do not possess it, it ought to be a matter of thankfulness that others do. But we have a different way of thinking. We court distinction—that I do not quarrel with—but we can *see* nothing but what has distinction to recommend it. This necessarily contracts our view of the Creator's beneficence within a narrow compass; and most unjustly. It is in those things which are so common as to be no distinction, that the amplitude of the divine benignity is perceived. The thirty-sixth chapter of his work on Natural Theology, entitled "The Goodness of the Deity," from which we have taken the preceding paragraphs, his biographer says, was "written under the pangs of the stone."

Solomon's opinion of the beneficial effect of cheerfulness is easily inferred, not only from the manner in which he commends it, but the frequency. *A merry heart*, he says, *doeth good like a medicine, but a broken spirit drieth the bones.* Or, as it is better rendered perhaps, in the old translation, "A joyful heart causeth good health; but a sorrowful mind drieth the bones." A fourth counsel, of incalculable value to those who would enjoy spiritual comfort, is to

BE TEMPERATE.

We refer not merely to the total disuse of alcoholic drinks and intoxicating drugs, which will be presumed, of course, but to that habitual control over every appetite which will keep us within the limits that are prescribed by both reason and health.

> Learn temperance, friends; and hear without disdain
> The choice of water. Thus the Coan sage*
> Opin'd, and thus the learned of every school.

In respect to drink, Dr. Johnson says "water is the only fluid which does not possess irritating, or at least, stimulating qualities; and in proportion as we rise on the scale of potation, from table-beer to ardent spirits, in the same ratio we educate the stomach and bowels for that state of morbid sensibility, which, in civilized life, will sooner or later supervene."

It does not properly fall within the scope of the writer to furnish such details as would

* Hippocrates.

be expected in a dietetical treatise, and which would come with more authority from an experienced physician. Burton, in his most extraordinary work called the "Anatomy of Melancholy," has given a curious disquisition on the intrinsic qualities of different kinds of food, and of their comparative tendency to nurture certain pleasant or painful affections of the mind, as well as animal propensities; but like many of the opinions of this eccentric writer, it is to be received with some material abatements. Dr. Rush, however, asserts that the effects of diet upon the moral faculty are more certain, though less attended to, than the effects of climate; that the quality, as well as the quantity of the aliment, has its influence; and that pride, cruelty, and sensuality, are as much the natural consequences of luxurious living, as are apoplexies and palsies. Fulness of bread, we are told, was one of the predisposing causes of the vices of the cities of the plain. He concurs too, with Dr. Paris and other eminent medical writers, both foreign and domestic, in reprobating the too free use of animal food by persons of sedentary habits, which not only predisposes to inflammatory diseases, but has a sensible influence on the morals. Dr. McNish, of Glasgow, quotes with approbation another opinion of Hufeland, that "infants who are accustomed to eat much animal food become robust, but at the same time passionate, violent, and brutal." It is said that a man living solely on beef, as the Indians generally do, and full of freedom and fresh air, has blood very nearly approaching, in chemical character, to that of a lion; the fibrin and red globules being more abundant, in proportion to the liquor sanguinis, and the temper of his mind approximates to the indomitable savage. When the Hon. C. A. Murray had been living for some time entirely on buffalo-beef, among the Pawnee Indians, his body got into the true savage training, and in the excitement and liberty of the wilds, he enjoyed the perfection of his animal nature. In describing the kind of intoxication arising from over-stimulating blood, he says, "I have never known such excitement in any exercise as I have experienced from a solitary walk among the mountains; thoughts crowd upon thoughts which I can neither control nor breathe in words." The efficacy of a vegetable diet upon the passions, was verified in the practice of Dr. Arbuthnot, who assures us that he cured several patients of irascible tempers, by nothing but the prescription of a simple vegetable regimen. Some devout persons, like Payson, have erred on the side of excessive abstinence; which his biographer pronounces to have been the great mistake of his life. To what extremes others have been carried under the influence of superstition, to mortify the body for the sins of the soul, is familiar to all who are conversant with the history of Asceticism; but the more common and dangerous error by far, is the opposite, or that of indulging the appetite too freely.

"When we contemplate each varying tribe of mankind, from the turtle-eating alderman to the earth-devouring Ottomaque, and see him subsist, exclusively or collectedly, on everything which air, earth, or ocean can produce, with, cœteris paribus, an equal degree of longevity, we are irresistibly led to the conclusion that it is principally by *excess* that we convert food into poison, and become liable to the attack of that Protean host of human miseries, called Nervous Diseases. Thus, Dr. Combe reasserts, with special approbation, the published opinion of a distinguished American physician, that intemperate eating is almost a universal fault; that it is begun in the cradle, and continued till we go down to the grave; that it is far more common than intemperance in drinking; and the aggregate of mischief that it does, is greater.

Plures crapula, quam gladius.
Gluttony kills more than the sword.

"For every reeling drunkard that disgraces our country, it contains one hundred persons who eat to excess and suffer by the practice." Baglivi, a celebrated Roman physician, mentions, that in Italy an unusually large proportion of the sick recovered during Lent, in consequence of the lower diet which is then observed as a part of the religious duties of the season. An eminent physician of London, writing on the influence of the luxurious habits of that great metropolis on the health of the higher classes, asserts that there is not one in ten whose digestive organs are in a healthy condition. This is proved, he says, incontestably by the tint of the eye and countenance, the feel of the skin, the state of the tongue, the stomach, and the bile.

Let the whole subject of dietetic economy then, be carefully regarded by those who are subject to spiritual and nervous depression; and while the conflicting opinions of the faculty, on the subject of diet or regimen, will abundantly show how "doctors disagree," yet they are, nevertheless, replete with suggestions of the highest practical value. It need hardly be remarked, that independent of the influence on the animal spirits and health, yet as prescribed by Christian morality, the appetites should be kept under habitual control. The spiritual man should learn, with the apostle

Paul, to keep his body under. He should live in that elevated state of communion with God, that he will not be tempted to descend from the higher and purer enjoyments of his religion, to seek happiness in the gratification of the epicurean and sensualist. But how far it is lawful to indulge a healthful appetite at his table from day to day, is a question of morals which cannot be settled for a Christian by any of the rules of medical science or physiology. *Put a knife to thy throat*, Solomon says, *if thou be a man given to appetite.* Restrain thyself, as if excess or repletion were death. But what may be received as at once the fruit of experience and the dictate of science, has been expressed in the measures of a writer not less gifted with poetic genius than with medical knowledge:

> ——— beyond the sense
> Of light refection, at the genial board
> Indulge not often, nor protract the feast
> To dull satiety.

Dr. Holland's three rules are: 1. Not to eat so much nor so long, as to cause a sense of uneasy repletion. 2. The rate of eating always to be so slow as to allow thorough mastication. 3. Use no urgent exercise, either of body or mind, immediately after a full meal. Rules," he remarks, "whose simplicity and familiarity may lessen their seeming value, yet in practice they will be found to include, directly or indirectly, a great proportion of the cases that come before the faculty for treatment." To these, however, he virtually adds a fourth, in a subsequent paragraph, in which he earnestly dehorts from the pernicious habit of directing the attention after eating to the region of the stomach, as tending greatly to disturb the process of digestion. To the question, How much ought I to eat? Dr. Hall says, it ought to be a sufficient rule for all men of common sense to reply—eat what you want, and as much as you want, and at regular times. But in the imperfect subjection to reason, instinct, and appetite, in which we find ourselves, a more definite guide is needed. The amount of food required differs with the different seasons. We need more in winter than in summer. It differs with the weather; more food is needed in a cold, damp, raw day, than in a cheerful, dry, warm one. Men require more food than women; those who labour, more than those who rest; those who are growing, more than those who have reached maturity. To lay down rules for all these, would require a better memory than would be exercised; and to weigh out the food to each particular case, would be attended with a very great deal of trouble. His opinion is, that in most cases, sedentary men in health eat too much, and that the necessity for so many hours of bodily exercise which many undergo, is a penalty for excessive indulgence of appetite. Doubtless a certain quantity of food is necessary to sustain the physical man in the vigorous use of his bodily functions; so is exercise not less needful for the twofold object, first, to work off and push out from the body all that is foreign, old, and useless; second, to replace these with strong, well-made particles; thus keeping the system clear of all rubbish, and replenishing it with what is new and perfect.

And yet it may be incidentally remarked here—and it contains a great practical truth—the less a man eats to a certain limit, the less he has to work off. Hence, those who eat little and work little, can study quite as much, and as advantageously, as those who eat a great deal, and, in order to get rid of their surplusage, have either to spend a large share of their time in working, or in washing or scrubbing it off with hard flesh-brushes—that is to say, for the few minutes pleasure of the passage of food down the throat, hours of otherwise unrequited exercise have to be gone through, or dancing under cool shower-baths, or the purgatorial application of hair-gloves or bristle-brushes. If literary men would drink only water, and eat one-half less, they could well afford to dispense with the fruitless exercises and penances just referred to. Few persons afflicted with despondency are aware how their malady is often aggravated by the occasional irritation of food or drink reacting on their mind by reason of the morbid sensibility of the stomach. Dr. Johnson says, "I have known many persons that found themselves so irritable after eating certain articles of difficult digestion, that they avoided society till the fit went off." Hence the rule that he gives to enable each person to decide his own case is, "any discomfort of body, any irritability or despondency of mind succeeding food or drink at the distance of an hour, a day, or even two or three days, may be regarded—other evident causes being absent—as a presumptive proof that the quantity has been too much, or the quality injurious." It is said, in the Life of President Edwards, that although of an infirm constitution and indifferent health, yet he was able to spend thirteen hours daily in his study. This surprising power of endurance is explained in the succeeding paragraph, in which we read that he carefully observed the effects of different sorts of food, and selected those which best fitted him for mental labour. Having also ascertained the quantity of food which, while it sustained his bodily strength, left his mind most sprightly and active, he scrupulously confined himself within the prescribed limits.

But not to dwell in details that are so accessible in elaborate treatises on this very subject, and that are deservedly held in the highest repute, we will only add, that the substance of what we have designed to say in the preceding remarks, is comprehended in an old Latin distich, by whom composed we do not recollect:

> Si tibi deficiant medici, medici tibi fiant
> Hæc tria; mens hilaris, requies, moderata diœta,

which one has paraphrased in the following clumsy couplet:

> Employ three physicians; first, Doctor Diet,
> Then Doctor Merryman, with Doctor Quiet.

Another counsel to be heeded with special care by the desponding, is to

Be habitually occupied.

We refer not to bodily exercise merely, so essential to vigorous health, and to a lively flow of the animal spirits, but we speak of occupation for the mind, in connection with some useful employment, to save it from those morbid actings by which it is made the prey to its own energies. Many diseases of body are produced, increased, and perpetuated by the attention being directed to the disordered part, but the employment which diverts the attention from the disease, often cures it. It is said that Kant was able to forget the pain of gout by a voluntary effort of thought; and paroxysms of his disease, that would have laid others aside, were scarcely heeded, while his mind was absorbed by some problem in metaphysics. We once knew an enterprising and successful man of business, who had hardly reached the meridian of his life before he had made a handsome fortune. He was now advised to sell his establishment, and live for the future more at his ease. The counsel was well intended; it seemed to be judicious, and was followed; but the sudden abstraction of so much care, by which his mind had been distended, caused a collapse. He soon became unhappy, desponding, and would have sunk into a state of melancholy but for the interposition of friends, who perceived at once his alarming condition, and the obvious cause. Without asking his consent, they re-purchased his place of business, and induced him to resume it. In a few weeks he recovered his former cheerfulness and mental energy. Employment gave a healthful stimulus to his mind, which suffered no relapse to its former morbid state through many years to the close of a long and useful life.

Whoever has noticed the amazing power of the thoughts in disturbing the functions of the body, will accord with the poet, that

> 'Tis the great art of life to manage well
> The restless mind.

This is none the less true in relation to religious men than to others. "There are many," Cecil says, "who sit at home, nursing themselves over a fire, and then trace up the natural effects of solitude, and want of air and exercise, into spiritual desertion. But this is to confound nature and grace, and to make a sort of mystery of that which is readily connected with a natural cause." Now and then we find one who appears to be happy in a sort of quietism, or cloistered piety, which rather shuns than seeks communion with what is without. How it will be in the world to come, we do not pretend to say; but it has never been found in this, that they are the happiest in religion who withdraw from all active occupation, and spend their whole time in devout contemplations. No man, it has been said, is ever more religious for having his mind constantly occupied with religion. This may seem a parodox, but those who know how little necessary connection there is between theological studies and spirituality of mind, and how much a professional familiarity with such subjects tends to deteriorate their influence, will readily subscribe to the truth of the assertion. Although the truly pious man can have but one dominant motive, the glory of God, yet the active powers of the mind will find useful and pleasant exercise in a thousand different ways of promoting it. To be engaged in doing good then, is alike needful to the happiness of the spiritual man and to his health.

Under a former head, we quoted one of four rules for the relief of melancholy Christians, and here we add another from the same author, viz. "to avoid idleness and want of employment; which, as it is a life not pleasing to God, so it is the opportunity for melancholy thoughts to be working, and the chiefest season for Satan to tempt us." It has often been observed in relation to clergymen who have been laborious and useful, that they ill endure a change to leisure from the occupation of a pastoral charge; but that in their *sine titulo* condition, they are apt to become either nervous and low-spirited, or turn to doing harm.

We were struck with a remark of Dr. Green, many years ago, on his retirement from Princeton, "that he did not know whether hereafter he should do much good; but he was resolved, if possible, to avoid doing mischief, which was more than was apt to be true of many of his brethren in similar circumstances."

To brood over our spiritual maladies, watching from day to day our changing frames, will no more help to attain a better spiritual condition, than the fingering of his pulse, or examining the tongue by the victim of dyspepsia will conduce to his more healthful digestion. In either case, the less he thinks of himself the better; and the only effectual expedient for diverting his thoughts will be found in some pleasant and useful occupation. Such was the relief which Cowper derived from his labour in translating Homer, and the poetical works of Madam Guion; and to find an antidote to his distressing melancholy was supposed to be Dr. Johnson's main inducement for proposing, towards the close of his life, to publish a translation of Thuanus. For the same purpose of turning his mind from its troubling meditations, he advised Boswell, who was as much given to despondency as himself, "never to speak of it to his friends in company."

"Were I asked," says a well known writer, "upon what circumstance the prevention of low spirits chiefly depended, I should borrow the ancient orator's mode of enforcing the leading principle of his art, and reply—employment—employment—employment. This is the grand panacea for the tædium vitæ, and all the train of fancied evils which prove so much more insupportable than real ones. It is a medicine that may be presented in a thousand forms, all equally efficacious."

We remember the case of a fellow-student in our theological course, whose mind was so disquieted with fears about his spiritual condition, that it became a serious question whether he should not renounce the hope of entering the ministry; but upon a statement of his case to one of his teachers, he was advised to discontinue his examinations of himself for a season, take it for granted, if he pleased, that his state was as bad as he feared, but to turn his attention to the case of others, pray more for them, and resolve to do all in his power for their salvation. This counsel was received, and was followed with the happiest results. His mind was gradually relieved, his spirits became buoyant and cheerful, and after finishing his studies, he entered the sacred profession with a joyful hope of his calling and salvation, which continued to the end of his life. Rev. Dr. Lobdell was at one time in a state of distressing doubt about three great questions pertaining to Christianity—Whether it was true?—Was he personally interested in it?—Had he been called of God to preach it? The very solicitude which he felt on the subject was evidence of his spiritual change, although he seemed not to know it. But instead of first undertaking to investigate the evidences of Christianity, then the subject of his personal faith and salvation, and, last of all, his call to the ministry, the process was exactly reversed. He first resolved to make it the purpose of his life to preach the gospel. "Then, and not till then, did he experience the preciousness of the Saviour to his own soul." His doubts and difficulties all vanished like darkness and mist before the rising sun. It was by *doing of the will of God* that he was made to know the truth of his *doctrine.* And so on in all his future life, whenever doubts and difficulties revived, they were removed, not by reasoning, but by losing sight of them in doing the will of his Divine Master. We would say, then, to every troubled believer, copy his example. Let not an elevated condition in life, and wealth, if you have them, tempt you to be idle. If not required to toil for your daily bread, yet let a regard for your happiness and health, and the monitions of conscience, make you as industrious as if you were. Consider your affluence and leisure as talents, by means of which you have the enviable opportunity of promoting the welfare of others, gratuitously, in a thousand modes, which are forbidden to others. Go join yourself to the most active benefactors of society; enter their ranks, or plant yourself in the van. Take your full share in the labours of the Sunday-school or Bible-class teacher, the distribution of tracts, the visiting of the poor and sick, and afflicted. Deny yourself many gratifications of ease, and pleasure, and advantage, for the sake of redeeming the time and the means of doing more good. Aim directly, like Harlan Page, at the single object of saving men's souls; and whether your success shall correspond to your wishes or not, you shall enjoy the reflex advantage of your benevolence. In watering others, you shall be watered yourself.

We are aware of the difficulty of complying with this counsel, in many cases, and none are more peculiarly trying than those of clergymen, who, from declining health, advancing age, or some untoward events, have been dislodged from posts of active usefulness, and have now nothing to do which is suited to their character, capacity, and circumstances. Such, it is well known, is often the unhappy condition of some of the most useful, as well as respectable and venerable ministers of the church; and it is one of the ominous signs of the times, that their number seems to be increasing. From the emoluments of their calling, few derive more than the means for a very frugal maintenance of their family, and therefore, when by reason of age and multiplied infirmities, *the grasshopper has become a burden*, they find superadded to all their afflictions the trials of poverty. We will not enlarge; but for ourselves, we are constrained to say, that we feel it to be a material defect in our ecclesiastical economy, that their condition and claims are not more particularly and tenderly regarded; that in view of the resources and benevolence of the Church, something has not been projected at least, if not carried into effect, by which such an important *casus omissus* should have been provided for, some feasible plan by which their remaining strength, their stores of learning and experience, may be turned to a profitable account, and these Mnasons of the ministry made happy and useful during the remnant of their pilgrimage. Persons subject to depression should

"WATCH AND PROMOTE BODILY HEALTH."

A counsel which we quote from a letter of the friend mentioned in our introductory note. We did not then know to what extent his sense of the value of health was suggested by the precarious state of his own. The influence of the body on the mental and moral faculties, shows the importance of a scrupulous attention to the former; to the use of all the means by which it may be preserved from any form of disease, and in the healthful exercise of all its functions. The fact cannot be impressed too deeply, that the connection between our sad and joyous emotions and our health is as inseparable as is that between the machinery of a clock or watch and the hands on the dial-plate: the movements which meet the eye are right or wrong, according to the condition of the wheels and parts that are invisible—

> Sine animo corpus, nec sine corpore
> Animus, bene valere potest.
>
> The mind or body ill, each partner feels
> The sufferings of the other.

On a subject of so much interest we have the teachings of many authors, some of whom not only weary by their diffuse details, but greatly perplex the mind by their disagreement among themselves. To those who need instruction most, and who have not the opportunity nor the time for much reading of this sort, it may be useful, at the risk of being thought prolix, to recapitulate and present again, in a connected form and with some amplification, a few of the instructions given very briefly in the preceding pages on the authority of Drs. Holland, Hall, Rush, and others, that enforce the "duty of health," such as

DUE DISCRIMINATION AND SELF-CONTROL IN RELATION TO OUR FOOD.

That we abstain from whatever is found to injure, and restrict ourselves rigidly to that sort and amount of aliment, whether animal or vegetable, which is most conducive to our general vigour and enjoyment, and which best comports with an active, cheerful, and sound mind in a sound body. Plutarch says that his countrymen, the Bœotians, were remarkable for their stupidity because they ate too much. They were good trencher-men, and good for nothing else. Let these and preceding hints on diet be properly heeded by the religious man, and his own experience will prove that his spiritual as well as intellectual enjoyment and usefulness are closely connected both with the quality and quantity of his daily food, and the right times for taking it. Richard Cumberland says in his Memoirs, Nature has given me the hereditary blessing of a constitutional and habitual temperance, that revolts at excess of any sort, and never suffers appetite to load the frame. I am accordingly as fit to resume my book or my pen the instant after my meal, as I was in the freshest hours of the morning.

GIVE BOTH MIND AND BODY SUFFICIENT REST, AND AT THE PROPER SEASON.

Not a small proportion of that despondency which is so incident to the sedentary class comes from excessive study at unseasonable hours. It is one of the "diseases of literature," to which good men are as liable as others. It is night study, Dr. Johnson says, that ruins the constitution, by keeping up a bewildered chaos of impressions on the brain during the succeeding sleep—if that can be called sleep which is constantly interrupted by incoherent dreams, and half-waking trains of thought. Physiologists have proved that periodical rest is necessary to the reproduction of that power in the nerves by which the will is enabled to act on the muscles. A due proportion of repose, therefore, is essential to the proper manifestation of mind in the orderly use of the body. We have known many remarkable cases of nervous disorder which were connected with this sort of imprudence. Night watching, or late sitting up, was reprobated in a doctor's Manual for the Nervous, written two hundred years ago, as tending to "tire and waste the animal spirits, by keeping them too long upon duty, debilitating nature, and thereby shortening the period of usefulness," according to the maxim,

> Quod caret alterna requie, durable non est.
> What would endure, must have alternate rest.

A theological student, who was about abandoning his studies in utter discouragement from declining health, was induced to forego his purpose until he had tried what could be done for him by a change of habits as to eating, sleeping, study, and rest. The new regimen proved so beneficial, that without the aid of drugs, by which he imagined his life had been sustained, he began to recover. In a short time his mind became cheerful, he regained his bodily vigour, and resumed his studies, which he afterwards prosecuted with equal profit and pleasure. It was the Rev. Dr. Miller's counsel not to study much by night. Begin with the dawn of day, and improve every moment of daylight that you can secure; but be extremely cautious of night studies. I have known them to injure incurably the eyes and the general health of many unwary students before they apprehended the least danger. Study, to a late hour at night, ought never to be indulged at all by any one who values his health. Two hours sleep before midnight are worth three, if not four, after it; and he who frequently allows himself to remain at his studies after eleven o'clock in the evening, is probably laying up in store for himself bitter repentance. A late writer ascribes the excellent health and mental vigour of M. Guizot, while Minister of France under Louis Philippe, to his "prodigious faculty for sleep." After the most boisterous and tumultuous sittings at the Chambers, where he had been baited by the opposition in the most savage manner, he was accustomed to go home, throw himself upon a couch, and fall immediately into a profound sleep, from which he was not disturbed till midnight, when proofs of the *Moniteur* were brought to him for inspection. It is well known that Henry Kirke White, Urquhart, and Henry Martyn, suffered at times from extreme depression of spirits, caused by an overtaxing of their mind, which occasioned the premature death of two, and probably abridged the life of the third. "My discoveries," Henry Martyn says, "are all at an end, and I am just where I was, in perfect darkness!"—a fitting sequel to the paragraph in his diary by which it is preceded: "I scarcely know how this week has passed; I remember, however, that one night I did not sleep a wink. One discovery succeeded another so rapidly in Hebrew, Arabic, and Greek, that I was sometimes almost in ecstasy." What effect could be linked to a cause more closely and inseparably than were the collapse of soul he speaks of, with his habitual imprudence in the violation of well-known physical laws?

Many suffer great depression of spirits from

the injurious effects of narcotics, especially in the form of tobacco. The name of ministers who use it, to the prejudice of their health, is legion. For this, and other reasons, some ecclesiastical bodies have made it a subject of discipline. Not long ago, a candidate for the ministry at the West was refused his license on account of his declining to give the habit up. Cowper greatly admired the Rev. Mr. Bull, of Newport-Pagnell, for his genius, literature, fine taste, and lovely temper—but, alas! nothing is perfect, he writes in a playful, but half serious letter, preserved by Haley, "the Bull smokes tobacco." In the famous "Counterblast to Tobacco" of King James the First, the custom of smoking is anathematized as "loathsome to the eye, hateful to the nose, paineful to the braine, dangerous to the lungs; and in the black, stinking fume thereof, nearest resembling the horrible Stygian smoke of the pit that is bottomless." In the time of Elizabeth, an edict was published against its use for fear lest England should become like the barbarians from whom its use was derived.

Anglorum corpora in barbarorum naturam degenerasse, quum iidem ac barbari delectentur.

Dr. Dunglison told the writer, that of the many cases of functional affections of the heart that he had seen, particularly among young men, a large proportion appeared to be owing to an immoderate use of tobacco. The accomplished author of "Letters on Clerical Habits and Manners," says that no class of persons are more apt to fall into excess in the use of tobacco, in every way, than students; and no class of students, perhaps, more remarkably than those who are devoted to the study of theology. Whether their sedentary habits, and especially their habits of stated composition, form the peculiar temptation by which so many of them are unhappily beguiled, I know not; but it has fallen to my lot to know a very large number of ministers, young and old, who by excessive smoking, chewing, or snuffing, have deranged the tone of their stomachs;

have undermined their health; have seriously injured their voices; have had the fumes of tobacco so thoroughly inwrought in their persons and clothing, that it became impossible for many delicate people to sit near them with impunity. They have laid themselves, after a while, under so absolute a necessity of smoking or chewing incessantly, that they have been obliged to withdraw from company, or from the most urgent business, and even to break off in the midst of a meal, and retire to smoke, or else run the risk of a severe affection of the stomach. In vain do you remind such people, when they are young, and when their habits are forming, that the use of tobacco is, in most cases, unhealthful, and in many extremely so; that if they use it at all, they are in danger of being betrayed into excess, in spite of every resolution to the contrary. They will not believe you; they are in no danger; others may have insensibly fallen into excess, and become offensive, but they never will. Onward they go with inflexible self-will, *as an ox goeth to the slaughter;* resolving to follow appetite at all hazards, until some of them become themselves fearful examples of the evils against which they were warned! The truth is, no man—especially no young man—ought ever to use tobacco in any shape, who can possibly avoid it; that is, who does not find himself reduced to the same necessity of taking it, as a medicine, that he is now and then of taking calomel; in which case, instead of allowing himself to contract a fondness for the article, and living upon it daily, a wise man will take it, as he would a most nauseous medicine, in as small quantities, and as seldom as possible. If the most servile votary of the segar, the quid, and the snuff-box, could take even a cursory glance at the ruined health, the trembling nerves, the impaired mental faculties, the miserable tippling habits, the disgraceful slavery, and the revolting fume, to which they have insensibly conducted many an unsuspecting devotee, he would fly with horror before even the possible approaches of danger.

But our venerable monitor reprobates the practice as not less a trespass against our neighbour than injurious to ourselves. I have known, he says, some persons who in consequence of their habitually chewing tobacco, or some other substance, or smoking, were under a necessity so constant and pressing of discharging saliva from their mouths, that they were really a trouble to themselves, as well as to everybody else. I have certainly known, at least, one tobacco-chewing clergyman, of whom a respectable professor of religion declared that he would most cheerfully pay his board for a week or more at a tavern, or at any other place, rather than endure his company at a single meal, or for one evening in his own dwelling. How melancholy, that a minister of religion, instead of being a pattern of neatness and purity, and possessing such manners as to render his company attractive to all classes of people, should allow himself, by his personal habits, to drive all cleanly and delicate persons from his presence! But the indulgence ceases to be a mere offence against taste, when we contemplate its havoc of life. According to the estimate of discerning physicians, not less than twenty thousand die in the United States every year from the use of tobacco. In Germany, where this pernicious habit is far more common, it is said that of all the deaths between the ages of eighteen and thirty-five, one-half originate in the waste of constitution by smoking. But in unnumbered cases where it does not destroy life, it exhausts and deranges the nervous powers, and produces some of the most distressing and unmanageable ailments. M. Bouisson, a French writer, has lately published some startling facts upon the danger of smoking. He states that cancer in the mouth has grown so frequent from the use of tobacco, that it now forms one of the most dreaded diseases in the hospitals. From 1845 to 1859 he has himself performed sixty-eight operations for cancers in the lips in the Hospital St. Eloi. The use of tobacco rarely produces lip cancer in youth. Almost all of Bouisson's patients had passed the age of forty. The disease is also more frequent with individuals of the humbler class, who smoke short pipes, and tobacco of inferior quality, while with the orientals who are careful to preserve the coolness of the mouth-piece by the transmission of the smoke through water, it is unknown; showing that it is generated more by the constant application of heat to the lips, than by the inhaling of nicotine. It is a common cause of disease in the stomach, and especially those forms that go under the name of dyspepsia, with all their kindred train of evils. It also exerts a disastrous influence upon the mind, and frequently produces an enfeebling of the memory, a confusion of ideas, irritability of temper, want of energy, an unsteadiness of purpose, melancholy, and sometimes insanity. These are the ultimate effects of the use of tobacco; and though one may not perceive them in his own case, we are assured that the tendency of the drug is always toward disease.

Much that is said of the evils of tobacco may be repeated of alcoholic drinks, and of stimulating or stupefying drugs. The practice of many, in their dejection from physical and other causes, to resort to opiates for relief, is as noxious to the health as it is immoral. Both Doctors Good and Cullen reject them as pernicious in cases of despondency. They seem to heighten the pressure of our malady only to let it hang upon us afterward more heavily. The way in which such agents operate injuriously, is "by disturbing the chemistry of life to such a degree that the nerve-matter no longer duly subserves its purpose as a medium through which the soul exercises volition, and perceives sensation." Dr. Moore says that narcotic substances seem to operate on the body by interfering with the affinity existing between the blood and the air, allowing the accumulation of carbon, or other noxious agents, in the circulating fluid, and thus arresting the action of the nervous system. On this principle, every kind of intoxication disturbs the voluntary operations of the mind by poisoning the brain, and thence impeding the influence of the will upon the circulation, by preventing its control over the nerves of sense and motion. Another indispensable auxiliary to health, is

Exercise in pure air.

The tendency of the depressing passions is to render us inert, taciturn, averse to society, and misanthropic. The languor and restlessness that usually attend this disordered state, make us unwilling to leave our retirement for the open air, or for the bodily efforts which our health calls for.

Ignavia corpus hebetat, labor firmat.

Indolence makes the body feeble, labour gives its strength.

It is not to be expected that in so limited a treatise as this, we should give a tithe of the excellent instructions or counsels which may be quoted to any extent from standard authors, in regard to the best means of preserving health, or for restoring it when impaired: what they say of diet, drinks, drugs, sleep, employment, bathing, riding, gymnastic exercises, walking, generous living, abstinence, &c. We merely allude to so copious a subject in this general way, to direct the reader's attention to what the wisest of them have written, rather than to any instructions of our own. But it ought to be specially noticed by the seeker after health, that while the disagreement of writers on the broad subject of regimen is notorious, they are in perfect harmony about the utility of exercise properly taken, and of wholesome air. One of their most distinguished authors says, if we would preserve our nerves in a state to favour mental exercise, we must insure our access to pure air. It is not enough to be guided by our senses in this matter; for unless we are supplied with fresh air at the rate of at least twenty cubic inches for every breath while tranquil, and twenty-five while in action, we shall be in danger. There is a great probability that the temper of an assembly is often vastly influenced by the state of the air which it breathes, and to talk of a moral atmosphere is not altogether a figure of speech. It is certain, that a crowded audience is usually most excitable at the commencement of a service, and the most attentive towards its close;

and it not unfrequently happens, "that at the end of a long sermon the flushed faces and hazy eyes of the congregation too often indicate that bad blood is adding its influence to aggravate the mental confusion produced by a disorderly discourse." Dr. Hall says, that "while exercise tends to abate disease under all circumstances, physicians recommend it to be taken in open air, in order to produce more immediate effects. The reason is, because a breath of air taken into the lungs, perfectly light and pure, comes out the next moment so laden with the impurity which it took from the blood, that it is a perfect stench, and would destroy life if breathed again; but coming from the body warm and rarefied, it ascends to regions where there is no animal life for it to destroy, to return to the lower world no more until it has been restored to its former purity." No persons better understand the value of these two helpers to a vigorous use of both the mental and bodily faculties, than some of our most successful scholars. In "Peter's Letters to his Kinsfolk," he gives us an amusing account of the boyish gymnastics of certain illustrious Scotchmen in the early part of the present century, who were wont to recruit their minds, after severe study, by relaxing in the athletic sports of youth, according to the advice of Horace to his friend Virgil,

> Misce stultitiam consiliis brevem.
> Dulce est desipere in loco.
>
> Mix a short folly with thy laboured schemes,
> 'Tis joyous folly that unbends the mind.—Francis.

The men that "Peter" speaks of, were most of them already beyond the meridian of life. "I was not a little astonished," he says, "when somebody proposed a trial of strength in leaping. Nor was my astonishment at all diminished when Mr. Playfair began to throw off his coat and waistcoat, and to prepare himself for taking his part in the contest; and, indeed, the whole party did the same, except Jeffrey alone, who was dressed in a short green jacket, with scarcely any skirts, and therefore seemed to consider himself as already sufficiently "accinctus ludo." I used to be a good leaper in my day, but I cut a very poor figure among these sinewy Caledonians. With the exception of Leslie, they all jumped wonderfully; and Jeffrey was quite miraculous, considering his brevity of stride. But the greatest wonder of the whole was Mr. Playfair. He also is a short man, and cannot be less than seventy, yet he took his stand with the assurance of an athletic, and positively beat every one of us. I was quite thunderstruck, never having heard the least hint of his being so great a geometrician in this sense of the word." We will only add to these suggestions with regard to exercise of mind and body, the counsel of one restored from prolonged melancholy, and who recites the teachings of his own experience. "Seek some suitable employment for exercise, and at the same time for diverting your thoughts from your trouble. Neglect, refuse, or reject this, and you have no ground of hope. If you are not confined to your bed, or if you can barely rise off it and walk, and this only at times, you should think of some useful, proper, and, if possible, profitable employment, at which you might do at least a little. In vain will you think and say, that you are too weak; all experience loudly exclaims—take exercise! take exercise!—if you can but walk or creep a little; and this especially to patients of your order. It is true that you do at times become very weak, but if you have no local disorder, or whether or not your weakness is of a peculiar kind; it will both come on and go off quicker than the weakness of patients labouring under other diseases."

While arranging our thoughts on the subject of this volume, we met with the following remarks of the Rev. Dr. N. L. Rice. They contain so many excellent counsels, reaffirming our own, that we are constrained to transfer them to our pages without change or abridgment. He is writing with special reference to his clerical brethren in their state of mental depression; but his suggestions are scarcely less adapted to the case of desponding Christians in general:

"There are some ministers and Christians who can say, as Dr. Daniel Baker said, 'I am always happy;' but there are many others who have seasons of depression of shorter or longer continuance, and of greater or less intensity. They are sometimes caused by some slight bodily indisposition, affecting the nervous system; sometimes by nervous exhaustion from loss of sleep or too long continued mental exertion; sometimes by disappointed hopes; and often by erroneous views as to prospects of usefulness, &c. They seem to be of the nature of melancholy, only they do not so generally create doubts of one's piety; and the causes being slight or transient, the mind soon recovers its cheerfulness. But whatever cause or causes produce these depressions, they are not only very distressing, but for the time being they unfit the mind for the discharge of any duty. We cannot read, for the mind takes no interest in any book, and wanders from what we are reading to its own gloomy imaginings. We cannot prepare a sermon, for the mind will not take hold of any subject. We feel, as we wander from text to text, that there is not a text in the Bible on which we could preach. We lose hours in the vain effort to choose a text, and then utterly fail to satisfy ourselves. We feel disinclined to visit; we do not wish to converse with any one, unless we can talk gloomily to some bosom friend. The pastor feels as if his usefulness were at an end in his present field, and half resolves to resign his pastoral charge. To those who are troubled with such depressions, as *we* have often been, we venture a few suggestions:

1. If it can be avoided, it is better not to attempt any mental labour whilst the depression continues. Whatever may be the cause, the fact is—the nervous system is *out of tune*. There is exhaustion and an irritable condition; and any attempt to force the mind to work will increase the difficulty; and the work, whilst doubly difficult, will not be as well done. Walk or ride out; breathe the fresh air, and converse with Nature. Vigorous muscular exercise, especially if at the same time the mind is amused, will often allay nervous irritation and depression. Or if there is general prostration of the system, and a feel-

ing of weariness, take half an hour's sleep; and you will be surprised at the virtue that is in 'tired nature's sweet restorer, balmy sleep.' Then a cup of good coffee will often make one feel like a new man. Often, when worn out with continuous preaching, we have found surprising relief from this source. All might not find the same benefit from it.

2. If it is absolutely necessary to preach under such depressions, two suggestions will be found important, viz. 1. Select a subject which demands, at the outset, *intellectual effort.* Depressions, such as we are considering, interfere far more with the *emotions* than with the *intellectual perceptions;* and if the intellect can get fairly to work in the effort to prove some proposition, or to explain some point of doctrine or duty, the emotions will gradually rise in the progress of the discussion, and the painful depression will entirely disappear. 2. Commence the discourse with the explanation of a word, or the statement of a fact or principle, and let the mind pass without special effort from thought to thought, and it will, in a few

minutes, work both vigorously and pleasantly. To select a subject which, from the beginning, appeals to the emotions, or is hortatory, or to commence at a point above one's own state of feeling, are both unsafe; for in either case the mind, instead of rising, sinks into deeper depression, and the preacher retires from the pulpit with the distressing feeling that he has made a failure.

3. It is unsafe to come to any new conclusions, or materially to change one's plans, whilst labouring under such depressions. At such times nothing appears in its true light. We are likely to err in regard to the state of feeling in our congregations; and difficulties, which at other times would produce no discouragement, appear insurmountable. In our own experience, once and again, an hour's sleep, a ride to the country, or a good cup of coffee, has removed mountains of difficulty, and driven away dark clouds that seemed to threaten ruin to all our plans of usefulness. The forming of important plans, which are to give direction to our labours for life, or at

least for years, requires a clear intellect and a manly vigour. It is often difficult, though it is most important, to avoid talking and acting unwisely in these fits of despondency.

4. There is little use in attempting to reason persons out of these gloomy moods. The effort to reason away a headache would be about as successful. The trouble is *physical;* the body is affecting the animal spirits, and thus obscuring the views and paralyzing the energies of the mind. It is generally even more unwise to ridicule the unreasonable conceits of persons who are low-spirited. Despondency is something strangely contradictory. It is very distressing; yet the mind nurses it as though it were a most delicious feeling. Ridicule appears unfeeling and cruel, and only fixes the mind more firmly in its gloomy state. If it can be diverted to some agreeable subject, the advantage will be very great; and a hearty laugh sometimes drives away all the demons of melancholy.

Some years ago, a minister from Virginia was lying sick at our house in Cincinnati.

He had nearly recovered; but, as it often happens, he had become very desponding, and seriously concluded that he should not live to reach home. Just while he was talking thus gloomily, our family physician came in. Discovering the desponding state of the invalid, he gradually turned the conversation into a more pleasant channel; and in half an hour he had the sick preacher laughing heartily. When the doctor left, he dressed himself, and walked about the house; and on the next day went on his journey.

Others, as well as ministers of the gospel, are afflicted with what is jestingly called *the blues;* and the suggestions already made may be of some advantage to them. A little timely rest and diversion will throw sunshine over the affairs of a man, which in hours of gloom seem desperate; and the Christian who is just ready to give up his class in the Sabbath-school, will resume his labours with cheerfulness."

In the fourth chapter of Dr. Alexander's "Thoughts on Religious Experience," will be found, among many wise counsels to persons subject to spiritual depression, some very striking examples, interspersed with judicious remarks. The importance of special watchfulness and prayer against the invasion of melancholy in the decline of life, especially when the tendency is constitutional, may be inferred from the cases of two persons who were overwhelmed with this malady at last, though as far from it in early life as any that the writer ever knew.

The first was a man of extraordinary talents, and eloquence; bold and decisive in his temper, and fond of company and good cheer. When about fifty-five or six years of age, without any external cause to produce the effect, his spirits began to sink, and feelings of melancholy to seize upon him. He avoided company, but I had frequent occasion to see him, and sometimes he could be engaged in conversation, when he could speak as judiciously as before; but he soon reverted to his dark melancholy mood. On one occasion he mentioned his case to me, and observed with emphasis, that he had no power whatever to resist the disease, and said he, with despair in his countenance, 'I shall soon be utterly overwhelmed.' And so it turned out, for the disease advanced until it ended in the worst form of *mania*, and soon terminated his life. The other was the case of a gentleman who had held office in the American army in the Revolutionary war. About the same age, or a little later, he lost his cheerfulness, which had never been interrupted before, and by degrees, sunk into a most deplorable state of melancholy, which as in the former case, soon ended in death. In this case, the first thing which I noticed, was a morbid sensibility of the moral sense, which filled him with remorse, for acts which had little or no moral turpitude attached to them. Let the depressed and desponding

LOOK HABITUALLY TO CHRIST.

A counsel, the most important, as it is the most comprehensive of all that have been offered. Look to Him continually for his ascension gift, the Comforter, to purify from sin, to help in overcoming *the world, the flesh, and the devil. Without me ye can do nothing*, says the Saviour; *and through Christ strengthening me*, says his great apostle, *I can do all things.* "Look forward to Jesus Christ," is the counsel of Mr. Rogers, "when you find things perplexed and troubled in your own souls; look to Him, and in the direct acts of faith, we have nobler objects to converse withal than when we look and pore upon our guilty selves. When we look into our troubled hearts, we can see nothing beside confusion and disorder there; but we may at the same time discern an all-sufficient fulness in God and Christ to relieve our wants. It is a long and tedious work to consider the several steps by which we are to proceed in such a case, whether we have believed or not; our duty is at this very instant to believe—i. e., under a penitent sense of what we have done amiss, to look unto Christ for help. We must carefully distinguish between justification and sanctification; between those habits and those holy actions that are the effects of faith, and faith itself. Our sanctification is full of imperfection; but that righteousness of Christ, wherein alone we are to trust for acceptance with God, is complete and perfect." Dr. Church, President of the Medical Society of Pittsburgh, Pennsylvania, mentions numerous facts to illustrate the efficacy of faith in Christ in the prevention and cure of diseases of body as well as mind. As health is the result of nicely-balanced appetites and passions, so of course anything that exerts a regulating or controlling influence over these in such a manner as to attune them into harmony, will essentially aid us in forestalling diseases, as well as in curing them. Such a power as Dr. Church ascribes to evangelical faith, would seem to be implied in the language of Dr. Bell, who says that "so intimate is the connection between physical comfort and moral well-being, that the one cannot be seriously affected without the other suffering." Mr. Shrubsole tells us in his Christian Memoirs, that he was once reduced so low that his case was apparently hopeless. For hours he was lying in convulsions, and during this time he was in a state of great spiritual darkness and distress of mind. But so soon as the light of divine truth broke in upon him, and he experienced the support of true faith, his convulsions left him, and he rapidly recovered. Dr. Church mentions the case of several sick persons of advanced age, who would probably have died under the power of these attacks, but for the perfect composure of mind and freedom from fear that were ministered by their faith. In view of the many facts concerning the remedial influence of faith alleged by other physicians of equal eminence, Dr. Ashbel Green takes occasion to combat what he calls a "serious evil." He refers to the "absurd, cruel, and wicked opinion," entertained by many physicians, and embraced by many of their patients, that a clergyman must be kept out of a sick-room—at least till the person is past recovery; an opinion which he avers was proved fallacious by his own experience in the pastoral charge of one of the largest congregations in the United States for more than the fourth part of a century, during which time he never knew an instance in which his ministerial visitations of the sick were apprehended, so far as he knew, to be injurious. What excuse then can be given, he asks, for depriving the sick of religious aid, when facts innumerable demonstrate that it may be afforded, not merely without harm, but often with evident advantage in helping the physician. The same sentiments on this important subject were entertained by his friend, Dr. Rush, who enumerates among the duties of a physician, "piety towards God, a respect for religion, and regular attendance on public worship." Without such moral endowments, he will meet with many cases of disease which he wants the requisite qualifications to treat. The sufferers need a medical counsellor who can point them to the *balm of Gilead*, and the *Physician there.* They must be directed beyond the remedy of secondary or merely physical causes to Him who can make them efficacious. And to mention all the cures that have been performed by faith and hope, he says, "would require many pages." But while the desponding look to Christ, and pray for themselves, let them seek an interest in the prayers of others. It is believed that the restoration of the Rev. Mr. Rogers, several times referred to in the preceding pages, was in answer to the special prayers of his pious friends and brethren in the ministry, many of whom were most earnest and importunate in their intercessions, till at length his mind was completely relieved. He has left a monument of this deliverance from his dreadful thraldom in a book well worthy of the perusal of those who suffer under spiritual distress from physical or any other causes. But the prevailing temptation of Christians of this temperament, as we have shown in another place, is to look to themselves, to watch their own fluctuating frames, canvass their motives and conduct, as if they expected to find the living among the dead. As if the Israelite in the wilderness, bitten of the fiery serpent, had depended for his recovery upon his former temperance, or the strength of his constitution, and not upon looking to the brazen image. Such reviews of the past and searchings of heart, are not only proper, but they are exceedingly important in many respects, but not for spiritual comfort in distress, nor for aid to arrive at assurance. To look back, as one observes, is more than we can sustain without going back. Indeed the better the Christian, the more spiritually minded and holy, the more does he usually discover to cause sorrow, and the keenest self-reproach, whenever he takes a retrospect of his past life and experience. For many years, we are told, that even Baxter was in great perplexity about himself, for reasons which have been a common occasion of doubting among serious inquirers in every age of the church: it was because he could not trace so distinctly the workings of the Spirit on his heart, as they were described in some practical writers, to whom he was directed for instruction, and he could not ascertain the time of his conversion. Because he felt great hardness of heart; supposed himself to be religious from early education rather than conviction of the Spirit; to be influenced more by fear than by love; and because his grief and humiliation on account of sin were not greater. But he was afterwards satisfied that these were not sufficient nor scriptural grounds for doubting his personal interest in the salvation of Christ. Upon which, Orme, his accomplished biographer, remarks, that persons who are agitated with perplexities similar to those of Baxter, are frequently directed to means little calculated to afford relief. It is very questionable whether any individual will ever obtain comfort by making himself, or the evidences of personal religion, the object of chief attention. All hope to the guilty creature is exterior to himself. In the human character, even under Christian influence, sufficient reason for condemnation, and therefore for fear, will always be found. It is not thinking of the disease, nor of the mode in which the remedy operates, nor of the description given of these things by others, but using the remedy itself that will effect the cure. The gospel is the heavenly appointed balsam for all the wounds of sin, and Jesus is the great Physician; it is to him, and to his testimony, therefore, as the revelation of pardon and healing, that the soul must be directed in all the stages of its spiritual career. When the glory of his character and work is seen, darkness of mind will be dissipated, the power of sin will be broken, genuine contrition will be felt, and joy and hope will fill the mind. It is from the Saviour and his sacrifice that all proper excitement in religion must proceed; and the attempt to produce that excitement by the workings of the mind on itself, must inevitably fail. Self-examination to discover the power of truth and the progress of principle in us, is highly important; but when employed with a view to obtain comfort under a sense of guilt, it never can succeed. Nothing but renewed application to the cross can produce the latter effect.

These sentiments are so important that they cannot be repeated too often, nor be too deeply impressed upon all, and especially upon every inquirer after an assurance of hope. They describe the only way by which the perplexed believer, even when released from the embarrassment of physical influences, can obtain a solid and permanent peace. It is by looking to Christ, not as holy in ourselves, but in order to be made holy; not as the *whole*, whose distempers have been cured already, but as the *sick*, who must be cured by him alone, or perish. We must go to him, feeling that we owe him ten thousand times more than we can pay; but that all he requires of us is to accept a discharge, and be happy in the enjoyment of this unmerited grace. In other words, we are only to exalt our glorious Redeemer to his true position as both the author and finisher of our faith, the alpha and omega in our salvation, and our peace is secured. Those very views of ourselves, our self-reproach and feeling of ill-desert, which have caused so much disquiet, then become the evidences of that spiritual change which is the beginning of everlasting life. It is as easy for God to forgive a thousand sins as one sin. If we be never so unworthy and so vile, yet mercy seeks no other qualification of its object but that it is necessitous, and liable to ruin; and it is a good way to fly to his mere grace and mercy, for we have undone ourselves. Poring upon ourselves does but increase our load. We are apt to say in our distress, "Were we so and so mortified to the world—were our hearts so purified and cleansed, then we might approach him with some boldness, who is altogether holy." This is true, but yet we must first ask of him to make us such, in whom he may delight. And as we sorrowfully cast our eyes upon our wounds and our miseries, let us look at the same time to that Physician who has provided a remedy for us by Christ, and who can heal all our backslidings, and teach us to apply that remedy. If we are the worst and most sinful creatures upon earth, yet is a Saviour tendered to our acceptance and our choice; and if we will receive him, all our transgressions, how heinous soever, will be blotted out. We repeat, then, the monition, in the midst of distracting cares and temptations, which so much hinder the exercise of this faith, let us not forget the promised help of the Holy Spirit. Let us watch against the common sin of the desponding, who undervalue his aid, and practically question its reality, when we are taught, not only that he *helpeth our infirmities*, but that *he maketh intercession for us with groanings which cannot be uttered.*

To know that we are Christians does not imply that we are free from sin, but that we are united to Christ. Our peace, and joy, and hope, the fruits of this union, need not be destroyed by our imperfections, however great, while we cling to Him as our righteousness. "If we see ourselves bad enough for Christ," Thomas Adam says, "he sees us good enough." His people are safe, notwithstanding their doubts and fears, not because of any inherent power in them to hold on to the end, but because of the grace which reigns in their calling and redemption, in view of which he has said, he will never leave them nor forsake them.

> The soul on his bosom that leans for repose,
> Is safe from the assaults of its bitterest foes;
> That soul, tho' all hell should its vengeance awake,
> He'll never, no never, no never forsake.

It is certainly among the deep mysteries of Providence, that some of the most eminent saints who have ever lived, should have been afflicted with despondency and gloom; and yet, as pious Rutherford remarks, "as nights and shadows are good for flowers, and moonlight and dews better than a continued sun, so is Christ's absence of special use, and it hath some nourishing virtue in it, and giveth sap to humility, and furnisheth a fair field for faith." But is there no difficulty, it may be asked, connected with the abandonment of a pious man to such a state of mental darkness and suffering, especially when protracted to the hour of death? No greater difficulty, we conceive, when viewed as the result of physical disease, than in a good man's being suffered to linger under a torturing complaint, or to be laid aside by paralysis, or to be the victim of brutal violence, of persecution, or of fatal accident. We know of no promise that insures a truly religious man against such a trial, although we believe the physical influence of true religion to be the very best preservative against those exciting causes which are likely to develop a predisposition to mental disease.

The history of Job is written to caution us against falling into the error of his friends in "so judging by feeble sense." It is true that he emerged from his complicated and unparalleled afflictions; but in the cases of diseases incurable, except by miracle, what reason is there to expect an extraordinary interposition of divine power, in anticipation of the blessed cure which death will effect when the spirit "bursts its chains with sweet surprise?" If Cowper was permitted to expire in apparent mental darkness, let it not be regarded as either militating against the divine goodness, nor as indicating the divine displeasure against the sufferer, should any one under similar circumstances be allowed to close his days under the pressure of distemper, and to give no sign in death.

It has been suggested, by way of explanation, that these sufferings of good men are designed to enhance the joys of heaven by contrast; that these light afflictions, which are but for a moment, will tend to *work for us a far more exceeding and eternal weight of glory.*

In many cases, moreover, they are made instrumental in furnishing religious teachers with a sort of knowledge that conduces greatly to their usefulness, and which can be acquired only by experience. The apostle represents our *High Priest* as one who could be *touched with the feeling of our infirmities, because he was in all points tempted as we are.* Such, according to the Rev. Dr. Hall, was the discipline which gave so much "sympathy, tenderness, and heart-reaching power to the discourses, conversation, and whole intercourse" of the late Dr. J. W. Alexander. To qualify him for this service, "the wise and gracious foresight of Almighty God saw it necessary to lead his disciple, from his earliest Christian walk, in the path of some of the most poignant and overwhelming distresses that can oppress the human soul. Ascribe it to what immediate cause we may—to delicate or disordered nerves, to morbid sensibilities, whether physical or moral; to excessive intellectual excitement; to preternatural susceptibility to the extremes of enjoyment and suffering, we know from the result that this part of experience—familiar to him, in a greater or less measure, from his youth to his last days—was the means sanctified to the production and maintenance of that depth, fulness, and richness of his spiritual traits, which laid the foundation of, and gave the predominant characteristics and direction to, his piety and influence. It has been said that God can bring affliction to try and manifest the graces of his people; as the stars, that are a chief part of the glory of the world, are then most illustrious and visible when the day is gone; and then he makes the sun to rise again, that displays new objects to us." The rods of God are many times very sharp, but at last we shall find that they were "dipped in honey, and managed with love." The conduct of Providence is always wise and good, but very often mysterious and unfathomable; and in nothing more so, than in his bringing 'abundance of his servants to heaven by the very gates of hell; and in suffering Satan to buffet and perplex them, that they may triumph over him in the latter end. He makes them to be in great perplexities, that the sweet wonders of his deliverance may the more appear. *We went through fire and through water, but thou broughtest us out into a wealthy place.*' God's people should be well satisfied, Mr. Rogers says, that He carries them to heaven in the way He thinks most proper. It were indeed a thing very desirable to be at ease, to travel with light about us; but if we must go through darkness, and danger, and calamity to heaven, let us be satisfied that his will is done, though we go weeping and groaning along thither. When his candle shines upon our tabernacle, we are well enough pleased; but when he begins to correct and chasten us for a season, we murmur, and think he is a hard master. But out of the ruins of the flesh, God raises the glorious structure of the new creature, and from the destruction of our earthly comforts he causes heavenly joys to spring. Let us not find fault with God's providence, for it will turn our water into wine, our tears of grief into the most pleasant joys, and, as at the marriage of Cana, we shall have the best at last. Two sorts of people, Dr. Watts observes, will be disappointed when they get to heaven—the melancholy Christian, to find himself there, and the censorious Christian, to find others there. But what can be deep or mysterious in Providence, or hard for us to believe, when we have once received that amazing doctrine of grace, the great central truth of revelation, that *God so loved the world as to give his only begotten Son, that whosoever believeth in him should not perish, but have everlasting life.* To many it is a subject of distressing perplexity, that persons of unquestioned piety sometimes continue to manifest great imperfections to the very end of their life. Even at the near approach of their transition from the earthly state to a heavenly, their sanctification seems to be immature. The mind of Dr. Guthrie appears to have been strongly impressed by this enigma in Christian experience, of which he could offer no other solution than that a change must take place at the moment of death, second only to that at the moment of conversion. "There is much sin to be cast off," he says, "like a slough, with this mortal flesh. Saw we the spirit at its departure, as Elisha saw his ascending master, we might see a mantle of imperfection and infirmity dropped from the chariot that bears it in triumph to the skies. I have thought that there must be a mysterious work done by the Spirit of God in the very hour of death, to form the glorious crown and cope-stone of all His other labours; and that like the wondrous but lovely plant which blows at midnight, grace comes out in its perfect beauty amid the darkness of the dying hour. How that is done, I do not know. It takes one whole summer to ripen the fields of corn, and five hundred years to bring the oak to its full maturity. But He, at whose almighty word this earth sprung at once into perfect being, loaded with orchards, and golden harvests, and clustering vines, and stately palms, and giant cedars—man in ripened manhood, and woman in her full blown charms, is able in the twinkling of an eye; ere our fingers have closed the filmy orbs, or we have stooped to print our last fond kiss on the marble brow, to crown the work his grace began. With him, *one day is as a thousand years, and a thousand years as one day. He shall perfect that which concerneth you. He shall bring forth the headstone thereof with shouting, crying, Grace, grace unto it. Now, therefore, unto Him that is able to keep you from falling, and to present you faultless before the presence of his glory with exceeding joy, to the only wise God our Saviour, be glory and majesty, dominion and power, both now and ever. Amen.*

INDEX.

A.

24*

PAGE.

D.

E.

PAGE.

H.

PAGE.

M.

PAGE.

S.

THE END.

www.ingramcontent.com/pod-product-compliance
Lightning Source LLC
LaVergne TN
LVHW020233110826
845151LV00003B/914